IN BREAD

LUCY HEAVER
AISLING COUGHLAN

Smith
Street
Books

INTRODUCTION

This book will not help you lose weight. But it will make you happy…

A sandwich is a wondrous thing. Fresh, simple and incredibly versatile, you would have to travel far to find a place that doesn't celebrate their own interpretation of this classic foodstuff. Food trends may come and go, but the sandwich remains, lauded for its ability to turn a few seemingly random ingredients into something unbelievably tasty.

Long before we became friends our first Saturday jobs were both in bakeries making sandwiches. There was something rather wonderful about spending a Saturday morning stuffing freshly baked rolls with as much filling as possible and seeing the smiles of happy customers as they walked out the door with their portable lunch.

Our appreciation for sandwiches was further cemented on a round-the-world trip where we were struggling to live off our self-allocated $20 per day. The answer soon became clear. Everywhere we went there was always something cheap and incredibly delicious to be had served in bread. Whether it was a torta from the streets of Mexico City, a chorizo bocadillo from a tapas bar in Madrid or the now world-famous banh mi from Hanoi, the sandwich became our sustenance of choice.

Since that trip we have been on a mission to document the very best fillings you can put in rolls, wraps, bagels and baguettes. This book is the culmination of our findings and it celebrates everything from the classics to global specialties to a few inventions of our own. You don't have to be a cook or a chef to enjoy this book; just a few ingredients and some imagination will get you by. The recipes are easy and great for feeding a crowd. They will also make you extremely popular. So, go forth, create, consume and most importantly, enjoy!

Here are our sandwich tips and tricks.

Sandwich layer etiquette

There are few things more disappointing than a soggy sandwich, but it doesn't have to be this way. 'Sealing' your bread with butter, mayonnaise or avocado provides a useful barrier between your ingredients and your bread. Placing something crisp on top will also help stop any liquid leaching through the layers. If you follow these simple rules your sandwich will remain intact.

What if I'm gluten free?

We completely understand that a cookbook on sandwiches might not be at the top of your wish list, but there are so many gluten-free bready options available today that it's super easy to swap out the bread in any of these recipes for a gluten-free version.

What if I don't have all of the ingredients?

Unless you're missing the actual bread, in which case stop reading this and get thee to a bakery, you can easily substitute most of the ingredients in this book. A sandwich's secret power is its versatility. Use what's available and try different combinations. You may find yourself a winner.

What if I don't like sandwiches?

Um...? We cannot help you.

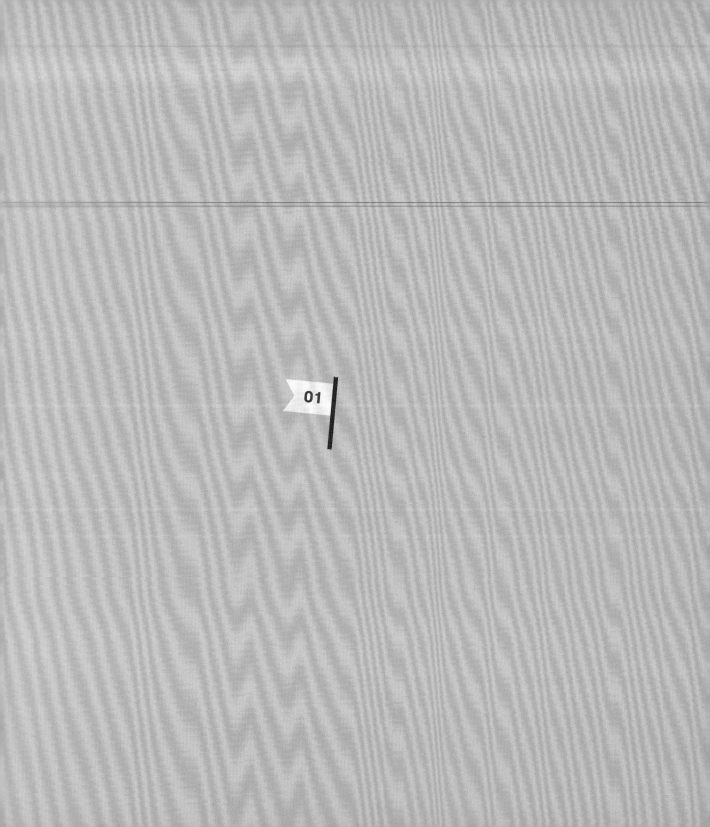

01

So much better than boring old toast and jam, these breakfast sandwiches make a seriously good start to the day. There's something rather brilliant about stuffing a cooked breakfast into a baguette and experiencing all that chewy, oozy goodness in one bite, while egg and sauce run down your arm. Perhaps more sophisticated are bagels, perfect portable breakfasts with no limit to their filling potential.

And if you sleep through breakfast, fear not as, quite frankly, these sandwiches should be enjoyed at any time of day. Brioche French toast is a completely legitimate dinner!

In Ireland, you can rock up to any decent service station, mini-supermarket or café and get your hands on a delicious breakfast roll, traditionally a baguette piled high with the makings of a full Irish breakfast, minus the baked beans of course. Choose your sauce, and be on your way. An actual hangover is optional.

THE HANGOVER — PART 1

SERVES 2

olive oil, for frying

2 pork sausages

2 slices bacon

6 slices black pudding

2 hash browns (frozen, ready-made is fine)

2 eggs

butter, for spreading

2 small baguettes, sliced open

tomato ketchup, to serve

1. Heat 1 tablespoon of olive oil in a large frying pan over medium heat. Fry the sausages, bacon and black pudding to your liking.

2. Cook the hash browns according to the packet instructions.

3. Heat 1 teaspoon of oil in a small frying pan and fry the eggs, also to your liking.

4. Generously butter the baguettes.

5. Divide the sausages, bacon and black pudding between the baguettes, then top each with a fried egg and a good drizzle of tomato ketchup. Season with salt and pepper to taste.

Vegetarians get hangovers, too! Yep, if you wake up feeling a little dusty from the night before, then this sandwich is the perfect cure. In fact, even if you're not hungover you should still make this sandwich. If it's warm outside you can cook it all on the barbecue, which is a rather lovely thing to do at breakfast. A bloody Mary wouldn't go amiss either...

THE HANGOVER — PART 2

SERVES 2

2½ tablespoons olive oil

1 onion, thinly sliced

small knob of butter, plus extra for spreading

1 garlic clove, finely chopped

2 large mushrooms, sliced

splash of soy sauce

6 × 1 cm (½ in) slices haloumi

2 hash browns (frozen, ready-made is fine)

1 medium-sized baguette, sliced in half, both halves sliced open

a few strips roasted red capsicum (bell pepper) (from a jar is fine)

1 avocado, sliced

small handful rocket (arugula)

hot sauce of your choice

1. Heat 2 tablespoons of the olive oil in a small saucepan over medium heat. Add the onion and fry, stirring regularly, for 10 minutes until well browned and starting to crisp. Remove from the heat and drain on paper towel.

2. Melt a knob of butter in a small frying pan over medium heat and add the garlic. Cook for about 2 minutes until the garlic is soft, then add the mushrooms. Increase the heat to high and fry for about 5 minutes until the mushrooms start to release their liquid. Add the soy sauce and salt and pepper to taste, then reduce the heat to medium and continue cooking until all the liquid has evaporated. Remove from the heat and transfer to a small bowl.

3. Add the remaining olive oil to the same pan over medium heat and add the haloumi slices. Fry for about 2 minutes on each side until golden brown.

4. Cook the hash browns according to the packet instructions and cut into thick strips.

5. Generously butter the baguettes and pile in the fried onion. Place the hash browns on top followed by the haloumi slices and mushrooms. Top with a few slices of roasted capsicum and avocado, and finish with the rocket and a few drops of your favourite hot sauce.

burrito comes from the Spanish word *burrito*, meaning donkey. Donkeys aside, you can shove pretty much anything in this sandwich. Here, we've opted for classic breakfast ingredients with a large helping of guac' thrown in for good measure. Wrap it up and you have a cooked breakfast, on the go.

BREAKFAST BURRITO

SERVES 2

2 eggs

splash of milk

olive oil, for frying

½ tablespoon butter

4 large mushrooms, thickly sliced

2 slices bacon (omit for a veggie version)

2 large flour tortillas

1 quantity Guacamole (page 172)

2 tablespoons pickled jalapeños

hot sauce of your choice

handful coriander (cilantro), roughly chopped

½ lime

1. Whisk the eggs with the milk in a small bowl and season with salt and pepper. Set aside.

2. Heat a little olive oil and half the butter in a small saucepan over medium heat. Add the mushrooms and stir to coat. Season with salt and pepper, reduce the heat to low and cook slowly for about 10 minutes until the liquid has evaporated and the mushrooms are starting to brown.

3. Meanwhile, heat 1 teaspoon of oil in a frying pan over medium heat and add the bacon. Cook until crisp.

4. Heat the remaining butter in a small saucepan over low heat. Add the egg mixture and cook for 2–3 minutes, stirring constantly, until scrambled. Remove from the heat.

5. Heat each tortilla in a large dry frying pan over medium heat for about 1 minute on each side until soft and warmed through. Preheat a sandwich press.

6. Spoon the scrambled egg onto one side of each tortilla and place the bacon on top. Add the mushrooms and a good helping of guacamole. Add the jalapeños and as much hot sauce as you can handle, then finish with the coriander and a good squeeze of lime.

7. Fold up the bottom end of each tortilla, then carefully fold over the shorter side and roll up. Toast the burrito in the sandwich press for 2–3 minutes until just starting to brown. (Spillages are subject to filling to tortilla ratio.)

Mmm, bagels. So delicious, so versatile, so perfect for breakfast. Whether you're in the mood for something savoury or sweet, the chances are you have something in the fridge or pantry that can be paired with these bready delights to make a delicious portable breakfast. We've included our favourite toppings here, but feel free to go *off-piste* and use whatever you have to hand.

THE LOX

SERVES 2

cream cheese, for spreading

2 plain bagels, sliced in half and toasted

100 g (3½ oz) smoked salmon, cut into strips

½ lemon

1. Spread liberal quantities of cream cheese on the bottom half of each bagel.

2. Top with strips of smoked salmon and a good squeeze of lemon juice. Add plenty of freshly cracked black pepper and place the remaining bagel halves on top.

SMASHED AVOCADO & FETA

SERVES 2

1 ripe avocado

juice of ½ lemon

2 multigrain bagels, sliced in half and toasted

50 g (1¾ oz) feta, crumbled

small handful seeds such as pepitas (pumpkin seeds), linseeds or sunflower kernels

1. Smash the avocado with the back of a fork in a small bowl. Add the lemon juice and season well with salt and pepper.

2. Spread the smashed avocado on the bottom half of each bagel and sprinkle over the feta and seeds. Add a little black pepper and place the remaining bagel halves on top.

BREAKFAST BAGELS

THE BLAT

SERVES 2

3 tablespoons whole egg mayonnaise

juice of ½ lemon

1 teaspoon olive oil

4 slices bacon

2 poppy seed bagels, sliced in half and toasted

1 large tomato, thickly sliced

1 avocado, sliced

small handful rocket (arugula)

chilli flakes (optional)

1. Mix the mayonnaise, lemon juice and a little salt and pepper in a small bowl.

2. Heat the oil in a non-stick frying pan over high heat. Fry the bacon for 2–3 minutes on each side until crisp or cooked to your liking.

3. Slather some of the lemon mayonnaise on the bottom half of each bagel and top with slices of tomato and avocado. Add the bacon and a few rocket leaves, then cover with the remaining bagel halves and serve with chilli flakes on the side, to taste, if using.

RICOTTA & HONEY

SERVES 2

large handful walnuts

100 g (3½ oz) fresh ricotta

1 tablespoon honey, plus extra for drizzling

2 cinnamon and raisin bagels, sliced in half and toasted

1. Preheat the oven to 170°C (340°F).

2. Spread the walnuts on a baking tray and toast in the oven for about 10 minutes until golden brown. Set aside to cool a little then roughly chop.

3. Combine the walnuts with the ricotta and honey in a small bowl, then spread generously onto each bagel half.

4. Drizzle extra honey over the top.

The story goes that French toast was invented as a way to use up stale bread – genius! It is so easy to make at home, we often think of it as a cheat's pancake. In this decadent breakfast sandwich, the fresh berries and the slight saltiness of the toast offset the sweetness of the Nutella. This is beyond good!

BRIOCHE FRENCH TOAST
WITH BANANA & NUTELLA

SERVES 2

2 eggs

2 tablespoons butter

4 slices brioche, cut 2.5 cm (1 in) thick

1 tablespoon brown sugar

2 large bananas, sliced in half lengthways

3 tablespoons orange juice

2 handfuls mixed fresh berries

2 tablespoons Nutella

icing (confectioners') sugar, to dust

1. Beat the eggs in a small bowl with a good pinch of salt, then pour into a shallow bowl.

2. Preheat the oven to 160°C (320°F).

3. Melt 1½ tablespoons of butter in a large frying pan over medium heat. Dip the brioche, one slice at a time, into the egg until well coated on both sides.

4. Carefully transfer one slice of brioche to the frying pan. Fry for 2–3 minutes on each side until golden brown, then transfer to the oven to keep warm. Repeat with the remaining brioche.

5. Melt the remaining butter in the same pan over medium heat. Add the sugar and the banana, and cook for 1 minute. Gently turn the banana over and add the orange juice. Leave for another minute to cook until just starting to caramelise.

6. Arrange the banana on 2 slices of French toast and top with the remaining brioche. Spoon over the berries and add a large dollop of Nutella. Dust with icing sugar and serve.

02

You may be tempted to skip this chapter if you are not vegan, but we promise you these are some of the tastiest recipes in the book. There can be so much more to a meat-free sandwich than a boring salad roll with limp lettuce and soggy tomato. With just a little imagination, you can create something packed with as much flavour as any meat or dairy offering.

Here, we've taken a few global classics and given them our own vegan spin. Don't be fooled into thinking these sandwiches are healthy, though. Cashew cheese, anyone?

TOFU BANH MI
WITH SATAY SAUCE

This sandwich is the mutt's nuts. Well, not literally, because then it wouldn't be vegan, but it is out-of-this-world delicious and packed full of umami goodness. Pass us the chilli!

250 g (9 oz) firm tofu

1 tablespoon olive oil

2 Vietnamese rolls or similar

½ quantity Pickled daikon
& carrot (page 169)

1 small cucumber, cut into batons

4 spring onions (scallions), shredded

1 small red chilli, thinly sliced

small handful coriander
(cilantro) sprigs

MARINADE

2.5 cm (1 in) piece ginger, chopped

1 garlic clove, finely chopped

2 tablespoons light soy sauce

1 tablespoon soy sauce

1 teaspoon Sriracha

1 teaspoon sesame oil

juice of 1 lime

1 lemongrass stalk, white part
only, thinly sliced

½ teaspoon sugar

SATAY SAUCE

125 g (4½ oz/½ cup) crunchy
peanut butter

2 tablespoons hoisin sauce

2 teaspoons freshly minced garlic
and ginger

juice of 1 lime

1 small red chilli, finely chopped

1 tablespoon light soy sauce

½ teaspoon sesame oil

1 teaspoon grated palm sugar

1. To make the marinade, whisk all of the ingredients in a large shallow bowl.

2. Cut the tofu into 1 cm (½ in) thick slices, add to the marinade and stir to coat well. Cover and set aside in the fridge for at least 30 minutes (it will keep perfectly for up to 24 hours).

3. To make the satay sauce, combine all of the ingredients and 2 tablespoons water in a small saucepan and stir over low heat until the peanut butter has melted a little and the sauce is well combined. Remove from the heat and set aside to cool.

4. Heat the olive oil in a non-stick frying pan over high heat and add the marinated tofu and a little of the marinade. Cook for 3–4 minutes until the marinade starts to caramelise. Flip the tofu over and reduce the heat to medium. Add a little more marinade and cook for a further 3–4 minutes, until the tofu is starting to crisp and the sauce has reduced to a sticky goo. Remove from the heat and set aside.

5. Split open the Vietnamese rolls and spoon in a generous amount of satay sauce. Add the cooked tofu and pile on the pickled daikon and carrot and cucumber batons. Top with the spring onion and sprinkle over the chilli and coriander to finish.

EGYPTIAN FALAFEL

SERVES 2

2 large Lebanese flatbreads

3 tablespoons vegetable oil

2 handfuls shredded iceberg lettuce

½ quantity Tahini sauce (page 173)

1 tablespoon Turkish pickled chillies

8–10 Pickled turnips (page 168)

2 Dill pickles (page 167), quartered lengthways

2 tomatoes, thickly sliced

FALAFEL

½ teaspoon cumin seeds

½ teaspoon coriander seeds

250 g (9 oz) dried broad (fava) beans, soaked in cold water for 12 hours

½ teaspoon bicarbonate of soda (baking soda)

½ white onion, finely chopped

1 garlic clove, finely chopped

small handful parsley, roughly chopped

small handful coriander (cilantro), roughly chopped

sesame seeds, for coating

1. To make the falafel, roughly crush the cumin and coriander seeds with a mortar and pestle. Drain the broad beans and rinse well, then transfer to a food processor along with the crushed seeds, bicarbonate of soda, onion, garlic and herbs, plus a good grind of salt and pepper. Blitz until well combined then transfer to a large bowl. Using your hands, form the mixture into about 12 falafel.

2. Cover the base of a shallow dish with sesame seeds and coat the falafel in the seeds. Set aside in the fridge for at least 1 hour to firm up. Pop any falafel that you don't plan to use in a zip lock bag and place in the freezer, where they will keep for up to 3 months.

3. Dry-fry the flatbreads in a large frying pan over high heat for about 30 seconds on each side, until soft and warmed through. Set aside and keep warm. Add the vegetable oil to the pan and reduce the heat to medium.

4. Add 6–8 falafel (or as many as you think you can stuff into your wraps) and fry for about 6–8 minutes on each side until golden brown and cooked through. If your falafel are a little on the plump side, you may need to press down with a spatula to help them cook all the way through. Transfer to paper towel to drain.

5. Place the shredded lettuce in a line on one side of each wrap. Sit the falafel on top and drizzle over lots of tahini sauce. Test-run a pickled chilli. Most Turkish pickled chillies are relatively mild, but if it blows your head off (as we have experienced way too late, way too many times), deseed them before adding to your wraps. Top with a few pickled turnips, the dill pickles and tomato. Add another drizzle of tahini sauce, then fold up the bottom of the wrap and roll over the shorter side, trying to catch all of the ingredients as you roll. Roll up completely and serve while still warm.

There is an Egyptian kebab shop around the corner from our house that makes the best broad (fava) bean falafel we've ever eaten. This recipe is our homage to them. The more pickles and tahini sauce you add the tastier it gets. Just don't go breathing on anyone for a while...

Sometimes the simple things are the most delicious things. Freshly made bruschetta, eaten outside on a warm summer's day is pretty hard to beat. Try to use the freshest ingredients you can find here to help the flavours shine through.

BRUSCHETTA

SERVES 2

3 large ripe tomatoes, roughly chopped

2 teaspoons sherry vinegar

pinch of sugar

1 ciabatta, thickly sliced

olive oil, for brushing and drizzling

¼ red onion, finely chopped

½ avocado, finely diced

1 tablespoon finely chopped parsley leaves

small handful kalamata olives, finely chopped

small handful capers, rinsed and finely chopped

1 garlic clove, finely chopped

a few basil leaves, to serve

1. Combine the tomato, sherry vinegar and sugar in a small bowl. Season with salt and pepper and set aside for 15 minutes to allow the flavours to infuse.

2. Brush the ciabatta slices with olive oil and toast in a griddle pan over high heat for 5–10 minutes until char marks appear. Alternatively, you can toast the ciabatta slices, but the flavour will not be the same.

3. Add the remaining ingredients except the basil leaves to the tomato mixture and stir well to combine. Pile the mixture onto each ciabatta slice and top with a few basil leaves and a drizzle of olive oil.

Our friend Helen suggested we include an ultimate salad sandwich in our book, and so the challenge was set. The key was to create something that was, yes, healthy but also as delicious as all of the other recipes. Enter, stage left, the ultimate salad wrap. OK, so it might not be *that* healthy, but why does vegan food have to be good for you all of the time? This is honestly one of our favourite sandwiches in the book. It is seriously good.

ULTIMATE SALAD WRAP

SERVES 2

4 squares mountain bread or similar

80 g (2¾ oz) cashew cheese

4 lettuce leaves, shredded

4 slices Pickled beetroot (page 168)

½ carrot, finely grated

½ avocado mashed with 1 teaspoon lemon juice

¼ red capsicum (bell pepper), thinly sliced

½ small cucumber, sliced

¼ red onion, thinly sliced

2 small handfuls alfalfa sprouts

Tahini sauce (page 173), for drizzling

small handful sunflower kernels (optional)

1. For each wrap, lay two squares of mountain bread on top of each other (this helps to prevent inevitable leakages, which will run down your hands and onto that nice clean shirt you just put on). Roughly spread the cashew cheese onto the bread and arrange the lettuce in a line on one side of each wrap.

2. Layer on the remaining ingredients, finishing with a large drizzle of tahini sauce and a sprinkling of sunflower kernels, if using. Season with black pepper.

3. Fold over the bottom of each wrap and roll over the shorter side, trying to catch all of the ingredients as you roll. Roll up completely and eat straightaway.

Lampredotto is an assuredly delicious and traditional sandwich recipe from Florence made with tripe. Try as we might, we just don't have the stomach (do you get it? Ah, I kill myself sometimes...) for this inner cow delicacy and so we decided to create our own version with slow-cooked mushrooms. I'm sure we would be reprimanded in Italy for such heresy, but we must admit it's rather wonderful and vegan to boot. Whether an Italian would agree with us or not remains to be seen...

MUSHROOM LAMPREDOTTO

SERVES 2

60 ml (2 fl oz/¼ cup) olive oil

1 shallot, finely chopped

1 large garlic clove, finely chopped

400 g (14 oz) mushrooms, stalks removed and caps roughly chopped

½ tablespoon soy sauce

3 tablespoons Pedro Ximénez Sherry

125 ml (4 fl oz/½ cup) vegan stock

1 tablespoon cashew cheese

1 tablespoon white truffle oil

2 large handfuls rocket (arugula)

2 round bread rolls, such as rosetta, sliced in half

1. Heat 3 tablespoons of the oil in a large frying pan over low–medium heat. Add the shallot and garlic and cook, stirring frequently, until soft and translucent.

2. Add the mushrooms and increase the heat to high. Cook for 1–2 minutes until the mushrooms start to release their liquid.

3. Add the soy sauce and cook for a further minute, then deglaze the pan with the sherry. Once the smell of alcohol has disappeared and the liquid has reduced, add the stock and stir to combine. Reduce the heat to medium and cook for 10–12 minutes until the mixture is a jammy consistency.

4. Reduce the heat to low and add the cashew cheese and white truffle oil. Stir well to combine – the cashew cheese melts like dairy cheese and will glue your mushrooms together into a rich coagulated gooey mess.

5. Transfer the mushrooms to a bowl, wipe the pan clean with paper towel and return to medium heat. Add the remaining oil and place the bread rolls cut side down in the pan. Cook for 2–3 minutes until the bread is lightly toasted.

6. Pile the mushroom mixture onto the bottom half of each roll and place the rocket and remaining bread roll halves on top.

03

Butter, eggs, cheese, mayo. There aren't many sandwiches that don't contain dairy in one form or another. And that's for good reason. The simplicity of a cheese sandwich, whether it's a ripe brie slathered on a French baguette or a sharp cheddar with pickle on thick-cut wholemeal is pretty hard to beat. And then there's the classic egg mayo, so perfect for picnics, or any number of sandwiches that are held together with freshly spread butter or mayonnaise.

This chapter celebrates all that is good about sandwiches that ooze, melt and squish. And remember, if in doubt, just add more cheese.

Ajvar is a Serbian roasted red capsicum (bell pepper) relish cooked with eggplant (aubergine), garlic, olive oil and vinegar. It is super versatile and pairs brilliantly with any number of dishes including meat, fish and pasta. It also makes a great dip and is often spread in sandwiches. Here, the haloumi gives a wonderful salty contrast to the piquant and slightly sweet relish.

HALOUMI WITH AJVAR

SERVES 2

splash of olive oil

6 × 1 cm (½ in) thick slices haloumi

butter, for spreading

2 poppy seed bagels, sliced in half and toasted

2 tablespoons ajvar

½ lemon

¼ red onion, sliced

large handful rocket (arugula)

1. Heat the olive oil in a small non-stick frying pan over medium heat. Add the haloumi and fry for 2 minutes on each side until golden brown. Season with black pepper.

2. Butter the toasted bagels and spread the ajvar on top of the butter.

3. Slice the haloumi in half lengthways and arrange on the ajvar. Season with black pepper and a squeeze of lemon juice.

4. Add the red onion and rocket and place the remaining bagel halves on top.

Ah, melted cheese in bread. Is there a finer culinary match? Maybe... Haute cuisine it is not, but a good grilled cheese sandwich is the epitome of comfort food – warming, indulgent and, perhaps, just a little bit wrong. There's no end to the cheesy possibilities here; the below recipe can easily be adapted, so let the contents of your fridge be your spirit guide.

THE GRILLED CHEESE

SERVES 2

50 g (1¾ oz) gruyère, grated

50 g (1¾ oz) red Leicester, grated

50 g (1¾ oz) cheddar, grated

butter, for spreading

4 slices white or wholemeal (whole-wheat) sandwich bread

PIMP YOUR CHEESE

1 tablespoon ploughman's pickle

2 tomatoes, sliced

1. Combine the grated cheeses in a small bowl and season with a pinch of salt and a good grind of black pepper.

2. Heat a jaffle iron/sandwich toaster. Generously butter the bread on one side.

3. Sprinkle the cheese on the unbuttered side of 2 bread slices and place the remaining bread on top, butter side up.

4. Transfer to the preheated jaffle iron and toast for 4–5 minutes until golden brown and the cheese is starting to ooze out the sides. Don't toast for any longer or the cheese will quickly melt through the bread leaving you with soggy bread devoid of filling, which would be very sad.

5. To take your grilled cheese toastie to the next level, add some pickle or tomato slices on top of the grated cheese before toasting. Warning: these additions will make your toastie one million degrees (scientific fact), requiring you to exercise extreme caution before tentatively taking that first bite. Enjoy!

Someone once asked a friend of ours where they could buy an egg sandwich. Her response was, 'the '80s?' Despite its retro reputation, a well-made egg mayonnaise sandwich is a pioneer in simplicity, often making a welcome addition to picnics, children's birthday parties and Women's Association conventions. The secret is to boil the egg until the yolk is just set but still slightly runny. This makes the mayonnaise mixture extra creamy and almost buttery.

EGG MAYONNAISE

SERVES 2

2 large eggs

butter, for spreading

4 slices multigrain bread, cut 2.5 cm (1 in) thick

2 tablespoons whole egg mayonnaise

small handful garlic chives, finely chopped

½ small cucumber, sliced

large handful rocket (arugula)

1. Bring a small saucepan of water to the boil and gently add the eggs. Simmer for 7 minutes – no more, no less – then drain and transfer to a bowl of cold water. Set aside for 10 minutes. Butter the bread.

2. Shell the eggs and smash them with the back of a fork in a small bowl. Add the mayonnaise and chives, and season with a pinch of salt and lots of black pepper.

3. Spoon the egg mixture onto 2 bread slices and top with cucumber slices, a pile of rocket and the remaining bread.

Fried green tomatoes are bloody delicious. If you grow your own tomatoes and find yourself with an unripened glut at the end of the season, this is the recipe for you. Not only do they make a fantastic sandwich filling, they also serve as a great vegetarian barbecue alternative to the often seen, sad shrivelled mushroom offering that loiters at the cold end of the grill, next to the burnt sausages.

FRIED GREEN TOMATOES WITH SLAW

SERVES 2

2 tablespoons polenta (cornmeal)

pinch of sugar

2 green tomatoes, thickly sliced

2 tablespoons olive oil

4 slices mature cheddar

butter, for spreading

2 crusty bread rolls, sliced in half and toasted

whole egg mayonnaise, for spreading

a few lettuce leaves such as cos (romaine) or butter lettuce

½ quantity Coleslaw (page 172)

¼ red onion, sliced

2 Dill pickles (page 167), sliced

hot sauce of your choice

1. Combine the polenta, sugar and a little salt and pepper in a small bowl. Dredge the tomato slices in the polenta until well coated on both sides.

2. Heat the olive oil in a small frying pan over medium heat. Add the tomato and cook for 3 minutes on each side until the polenta is golden brown all over. Remove from the heat and set aside to drain on paper towel. Place the cheese slices on top of the tomato so they melt a little.

3. Generously butter the bottom half of each roll and spread mayonnaise on the top halves. Place a few lettuce leaves on the butter, then top with a good amount of slaw and add the fried tomato. Finish with a few slices of red onion and dill pickle and drizzle over a few drops of your favourite hot sauce.

This variation on the red, white and green Italian salad is super quick and makes the most of a few good quality ingredients. If you're feeling the need to add some protein, pile a few slices of prosciutto or salami on top. You can toast the bread in a frying pan instead of on a griddle, but you won't achieve that delicious charred, smoky flavour.

CAPRESE WITH BALSAMIC GLAZE

SERVES 2

2 ciabatta rolls, sliced in half

olive oil, for brushing

1 garlic clove, cut in half

3–4 tomatoes, thickly sliced

2 balls fresh buffalo mozzarella, sliced

a few basil leaves

BALSAMIC GLAZE
250 ml (8½ fl oz/1 cup) balsamic vinegar

1. To make the balsamic glaze, place the vinegar in a small saucepan over high heat and bring to the boil. Reduce the heat to low and simmer for about 20 minutes or until the vinegar has reduced by half and coats the back of a spoon.

2. Preheat a griddle pan to high.

3. Brush the cut sides of the ciabatta with olive oil then rub with the garlic. Place the ciabatta halves cut side down in the griddle pan and toast until char marks appear. This can take anywhere up to 10 minutes. Placing a plate on top of the ciabatta will help speed up this process and prevent your kitchen from filling up with smoke.

4. Layer slices of tomato and mozzarella on the bottom half of each ciabatta. Tear over a few basil leaves, then season with salt and plenty of cracked black pepper, and a drizzle of the balsamic glaze.

Every English pub worth its salt sells a variation of the classic Ploughman's lunch. Cheese, meat, crunchy pickles, salad and possibly a few salted crisps on the side, all washed down with a pint of beer is simple but deliriously enjoyable. Here, we've put the ingredients in a doorstep sandwich, another great English pub culinary feat. We've made this sandwich vegetarian, but by all means throw in some ham if you want to go the whole hog.

THE PLOUGHMAN'S DOORSTEP

SERVES 2

2 tablespoons ploughman's pickle (sorry to name-drop, but Branston is the best)

4 slices white or wholemeal (whole-wheat) bread, cut 2.5 cm (1 in) thick

whole egg mayonnaise, for spreading

70 g (2½ oz) mature cheddar (the bitier the better), sliced

2 large pickled onions, sliced

a few cos (romaine) lettuce leaves

2 tomatoes, thickly sliced

½ small cucumber, sliced

salted crisps (potato chips), to serve

1. Spread the pickle on 2 slices of bread and some mayonnaise on the other 2 slices.

2. Lay the sliced cheddar on top of the pickle and add the pickled onions. Place a few lettuce leaves on top, followed by the tomato and cucumber slices. Season with salt and pepper and top with the remaining bread.

3. Serve with salted crisps on the side, preferably in a 14th century pub in England, with an open fire, a hopeful Labrador and a rosy-cheeked barman.

There's been some debate about the use of the term rabbit vs rarebit. Rabbit came first, but rarebit seems to be more widely used. Rabbit or rarebit, however you say it, there's no bunny in this recipe.

WELSH RAREBIT [OR IS THAT RABBIT?]

SERVES 2

30 g (1 oz) butter

60 ml (2 fl oz/¼ cup) pale ale or stout

3 teaspoons Coleman's English mustard

15 g (½ oz) plain (all-purpose) flour

140 g (5 oz) mature cheddar, grated

4 slices white or wholemeal (whole-wheat) bread, cut 2.5 cm (1 in) thick

2 egg yolks

Worcestershire sauce, for drizzlilng (optional)

1. Melt the butter in a small saucepan over low heat. Add the ale or stout, mustard and flour, and cook, stirring, for 1–2 minutes. Add the cheese and stir slowly until melted. Remove from the heat and set aside to cool a little.

2. Preheat a grill (broiler) to high. Toast the bread on both sides.

3. Add the egg yolks one at a time to the cheese mixture and mix until smooth. Spoon the mixture evenly over the toasted bread, smoothing out right to the edges to avoid burnt crusts.

4. Grill until bubbling. Serve immediately drizzled with Worcestershire sauce, if desired.

When you wake up in the morning and the first thought that enters your head is 'I'm never drinking again', this is the sandwich to reach for. It contains all the goodness (badness) you need to make you feel human again. Now, slowly make your way to the kitchen, shove the ingredients between the bread, then retreat to your cave of shame, while contemplating what you did the previous night. You can thank me later.

CHEDDAR, PICKLED ONIONS & CRISPS

SERVES 2

butter, for spreading

4 slices white bread, cut 2.5 cm (1 in) thick

125 g (4½ oz) mature cheddar, grated

4 medium-sized pickled onions, sliced

salted crisps (potato chips), or flavour of your choice

1. Butter the bread and sprinkle the cheese over 2 slices.

2. Sit the pickled onion on top, then pile on as many crisps that you think will fit in your mouth.

3. Top with the remaining bread and consume with something cold, fizzy and non-alcoholic (although, this would probably taste awesome with a glass of champagne if you're brave enough for a hair-of-the-dog).

THE BLACK BEAN WRAP

SERVES 2

DAIRY

2 large flour tortillas

60 g (2 oz) sour cream

60 g (2 oz) grated cheddar

½ quantity Guacamole (page 172)

shredded butter lettuce leaves

a few slices Pickled red onion
(page 169)

2 tablespoons pickled jalapeños

a few coriander (cilantro) leaves

green or red habanero hot sauce

BLACK BEANS

100 g (3½ oz) dried black beans,
soaked in cold water overnight

3 tablespoons olive oil

1 onion, chopped

2 garlic cloves, finely chopped

1 celery stalk, finely chopped

½ red capsicum (bell pepper),
finely chopped

2 teaspoons smoked paprika

1 teaspoon ground cumin

½ teaspoon cayenne pepper

1 teaspoon ground coriander

½ teaspoon dried oregano

1 tomato, roughly chopped

1 chipotle in adobo sauce

2 teaspoons adobo sauce

400 g (14 oz) tin tomatoes

juice of 1 lime

3 spring onions (scallions), sliced

½ teaspoon salt

1½ teaspoons sugar

1. To make the black beans, drain the beans and rinse well. Transfer to a large saucepan and cover with cold water. Bring to the boil then simmer for about 45 minutes until tender. Drain and set aside.

2. Heat the oil in a large saucepan over medium heat. Add the onion and fry, stirring regularly, for to 2–3 minutes until translucent. Add the garlic and cook for a further minute. Add the celery and capsicum and stir well to combine. Reduce the heat a little and cook slowly for about 10 minutes until the vegetables are soft and have sweated out their juices.

3. Increase the heat to medium and add the spices and dried oregano. Cook, stirring, until the smells fill the room, then add the tomato and the chipotle and adobo sauce. Cook for a few more minutes, until the tomato starts to break down, then add the tinned tomatoes and a tinful of water. Stir through the beans then reduce the heat to low and leave to cook, stirring occasionally, for about 90 minutes until reduced and thick.

4. Add the lime juice, spring onion, salt and sugar along with a good grind of black pepper. Stir well and check the seasoning – it should be slightly sweet, salty and fresh-tasting while being thoroughly warming at the same time.

5. Dry-fry the tortillas in a large frying pan over high heat for about 30 seconds on each side, until soft and warmed through. Preheat a sandwich press.

6. Smear the sour cream on the tortillas and place 3 tablespoons of black beans on one side of each tortilla. Sprinkle the cheese over the top and arrange the guacamole to one side of the beans. Top with the lettuce, pickled onion slices, jalapeños and coriander, and drizzle with hot sauce at your own discretion.

7. Fold up the bottom half of each wrap and roll over the shorter side, trying to catch all of the ingredients as you roll. Continue rolling into a wrap, then toast in the sandwich press for 1–2 minutes. Serve with extra hot sauce.

Don't be put off by the length of this recipe; once you've made the beans it's very quick to put together, and the beans will keep for up to a week in the fridge. Nachos anyone? Look, we'll even keep this intro short so you can get started.

Pav bhaji is a delicious local street food from Mumbai consisting of a hot buttered roll slathered in a mashed vegetable gravy – it's almost like a curried sloppy Joe. There are many variations but we've gone with a classic version here, topped with white onion and lots of lemon juice. The pav masala will keep in the pantry for up to three months.

PAV BHAJI

SERVES 2

1 large potato, roughly chopped

½ carrot, roughly chopped

large handful frozen peas

60 g (2 oz) butter

1 small onion, finely chopped

1 garlic clove, finely chopped

1 teaspoon grated ginger

1 green chilli, finely chopped

½ green capsicum (bell pepper), roughly chopped

2 tomatoes, roughly chopped

1 tablespoon pav masala

½ teaspoon garam masala

½ teaspoon ground turmeric

1 dried red chilli, finely chopped

2 teaspoons salt

2 soft white rolls, cut in half

½ white onion, thinly sliced

small handful coriander (cilantro), roughly chopped

lemon wedges, to serve

PAV MASALA

8 dried red chillies

4 cloves

5 cm (2 in) stick cinnamon

3 tablespoons coriander seeds

1 tablespoon cumin seeds

3 teaspoons black peppercorns

1 tablespoon fennel seeds

1 tablespoon amchur powder

½ tablespoon ground turmeric

1. To make the pav masala, dry-roast the whole spices for 4–5 minutes until they are lightly toasted. Remove from the heat and set aside to cool a little, then transfer to a spice grinder and add the amchur powder and ground turmeric. Blitz until you have a fine powder.

2. Bring the potato to the boil in a large saucepan of salted water and simmer for 7–10 minutes until soft. Remove the potato with a slotted spoon and transfer to a large bowl. Add the carrot to the saucepan and simmer for 5 minutes. Add the peas and simmer for a further 2 minutes. Drain and set aside in another bowl.

3. Heat half the butter in a large frying pan over medium heat. Add the onion and cook, stirring frequently, for 2–3 minutes until translucent. Roughly pound the garlic and ginger with a mortar and pestle, then add to the pan and cook for a further 2 minutes. Add the green chilli and continue cooking for another minute, then add the capsicum. Stir everything to combine then add the tomato and mix well. Cook for 2 minutes then add the pav masala, spices and salt. Continue cooking for 6–7 minutes until the tomato has completely collapsed and you are left with a thickish paste. Add 375 ml (12½ fl oz/1½ cups) water and stir to combine.

4. Mash the potato until smooth. Roughly smash the carrot and peas. Add the potato and vegetables to the pan and mix well. Add half of the remaining butter and simmer for 10–15 minutes until thick and creamy. Transfer to a bowl and keep warm.

5. Wipe the pan clean and melt the remaining butter over medium heat. Place the cut sides of each roll in the pan and cook for 5–6 minutes until the bread has soaked up the butter and the undersides are toasted.

6. Heap the curry mixture onto the cut rolls and serve with slices of white onion, coriander and lemon wedges.

Raclette is a much-loved Swiss cheese that's having a bit of a moment. Although it has been around for centuries, raclette is only now appearing on restaurant menus outside of France and Switzerland. Traditionally, the cheese is melted over an open fire, then scraped directly from the wheel onto a pile of baby potatoes and chopped gherkins, and maybe some thinly sliced meat. We've made a deconstructed reconstructed version here by adding bread into the mix. Just don't plan on doing any vigorous exercise afterwards.

RACLETTE & POTATO WITH A PICKLE

SERVES 2

3 kipfler or new potatoes
100 g (3½ oz) raclette, grated
4 slices white bread, cut 2.5 cm (1 in) thick
butter, for spreading
2 Dill pickles (page 167)

1. Boil the potatoes in plenty of salted boiling water until just tender. Drain and set aside to cool slightly, then slice into thin rounds. Quickly combine with the grated raclette and season to taste (you want the potato to slightly melt the cheese).

2. Preheat a sandwich press.

3. Toast one side of each bread slice, then top 2 slices with the potato mixture. Cover with the remaining bread, toast side down.

4. Generously butter the untoasted sides of bread, then transfer to the sandwich press and toast until golden brown.

5. Spear the dill pickles with a toothpick, then place on top of your sandwich.

Muffuletta is the name given to a type of bread brought over to Louisiana by Italian immigrants. The name also applies to this sandwich, which is traditionally filled with an olive salad and as much deli meat and cheese as you can squeeze in. The olive salad is extremely addictive and is a fantastic accompaniment to a cheese board or served with fish. You need to make it the day before to allow the flavours to develop. We recommend making double the quantity so you have leftovers.

MUFFULETTA

1 × 800 g (1 lb 12 oz) Italian sourdough cob loaf, or similar

80 g (2¾ oz) sliced ham

60 g (2 oz) sliced mild salami

60 g (2 oz) hot sopressa

6 slices provolone

OLIVE SALAD

12 extra-large green pitted olives, roughly chopped

8 black olives, roughly chopped

20 pimentos, roughly chopped

1 celery stalk, finely diced

1 carrot, finely diced

2 garlic cloves, finely chopped

1 tablespoon capers, rinsed and chopped

small handful finely chopped parsley

1 teaspoon dried oregano

1 teaspoon dried thyme

90 ml (3 fl oz) olive oil

juice of 1 lemon

2 tablespoons red wine vinegar

1. Make the olive salad a day ahead. Combine all of the ingredients in a medium-sized bowl and season with a pinch of salt and lots of black pepper. Transfer to an airtight container and refrigerate overnight.

2. Slice the top third off the cob loaf and pull out two-thirds of the bread from the inside and a little from the 'lid'. Blitz into breadcrumbs and place in the freezer for another use.

3. Give the olive salad a good stir then spread about half into the bottom of your bread 'bowl'. Top with a layer each of sliced ham, salami, hot sopressa and provolone. Repeat the meat and cheese layers and finish with the remaining olive salad (you should still be able to put the sandwich 'lid' on tightly). Add the top of the bread and wrap the whole lot tightly in plastic wrap.

4. Set aside for a couple of hours so the olive oil soaks into the bread. Divide the cob into four triangles and serve.

HIGH TEA SANDWICHES

So dainty, so pretty, who doesn't love a high tea sandwich? Bring some posh into your life and pretend you're at the Ritz drinking endless Champagne served to you by a waiter named Byron while guffawing over the state of social media in the digital age. It'll be just like the old days...

CUCUMBER

SERVES 4

butter, for spreading

8 slices white sandwich bread

cream cheese, for spreading

½ small cucumber, thinly sliced

1. Butter 4 slices of bread and spread cream cheese on the remaining 4 slices.

2. Place the cucumber slices on top of the cream cheese and season with salt and pepper. Top with the buttered bread, remove the crusts and cut into fingers.

SMOKED SALMON

SERVES 4

butter, for spreading

8 slices wholemeal (whole-wheat) sandwich bread

4 slices smoked salmon

1 lemon, halved

1. Generously butter the bread and place a slice of smoked salmon on 4 slices.

2. Squeeze over some lemon juice and grind over lots of black pepper. Top with the remaining bread slices, remove the crusts and cut into fingers.

CHICKEN & MAYONNAISE

SERVES 4

350 g (12½ oz) poached/
barbecued chicken breast,
shredded

60 g (2 oz/¼ cup) whole
egg mayonnaise

3 spring onions (scallions),
thinly sliced

butter, for spreading

8 slices white sandwich
bread

4 butter lettuce leaves

1. Combine the chicken, mayonnaise and spring onion in
   a small bowl. Season with salt and pepper.

2. Butter the bread.

3. Spread the mixture on 4 slices of bread and top with
   a lettuce leaf. Top with the remaining bread slices, remove
   the crusts and cut into triangles.

SMOKED TROUT

SERVES 4

200 g (7 oz) hot smoked
trout, flaked

2 heaped teaspoons grated
horseradish

2 tablespoons crème fraîche

2 tablespoons cream cheese

juice of 1 lemon

1 tablespoon finely
chopped dill

butter, for spreading

8 slices wholemeal (whole-
wheat) sandwich bread

large handful watercress,
roughly chopped

1. Combine the smoked trout, horseradish, crème fraîche,
   cream cheese, lemon juice and dill in a small bowl. Season
   with pepper.

2. Butter the bread.

3. Spread the trout mixture on 4 slices and top with the
   watercress. Add the remaining bread slices, remove
   the crusts and cut into triangles.

04

Tuna sandwiches are a regular feature in office lunch boxes the world over, but there is so much more to a fish sandwich than this rather pungent filling. Multiple interpretations of fresh fish served in bread are celebrated along coastal regions, usually containing nothing more than just-caught seafood, crisp salad and a creamy sauce, allowing the simple flavours to shine through.

Their simplicity is reflected in these recipes, which are quick to make and fantastic for feeding a crowd. Does it really get any better than lobster in a roll?

Behold the lobster roll! Perhaps the king of all sandwiches. The epitome of *In Bread* chic. Whoever came up with the idea of shoving freshly cooked lobster into a hot buttered roll was on to a very good thing. This simple recipe allows the flavours to speak for themselves, and we haven't ventured too far from the original because why mess with perfection?

THE NEW ENGLAND LOBSTER ROLL

SERVES 2

butter, for spreading

2 long soft rolls, tops split open lengthways

½ celery stalk, thinly sliced

a few snipped chives

juice of ½ lemon

1 tablespoon whole egg mayonnaise

2 cooked lobster tails or crayfish, flesh chopped into bite-sized pieces

small handful watercress

1. Slather butter on the outside of each roll (stay with me here). Heat a large frying pan over medium heat and add the buttered rolls. Lightly toast until the butter has melted and your rolls look like they've had a spray-tan. Remove from the heat and set aside.

2. Combine the celery, chives, lemon juice and mayonnaise in a small bowl. (Resist the temptation to add more mayo. If you're spending the money on making a lobster sandwich you want to be able to taste the damn thing). Season with the tiniest bit of salt and lots of black pepper. Stir through the chopped lobster and check the seasoning.

3. Pile the lobster mixture into the rolls and add a few watercress stalks for colour and crunch.

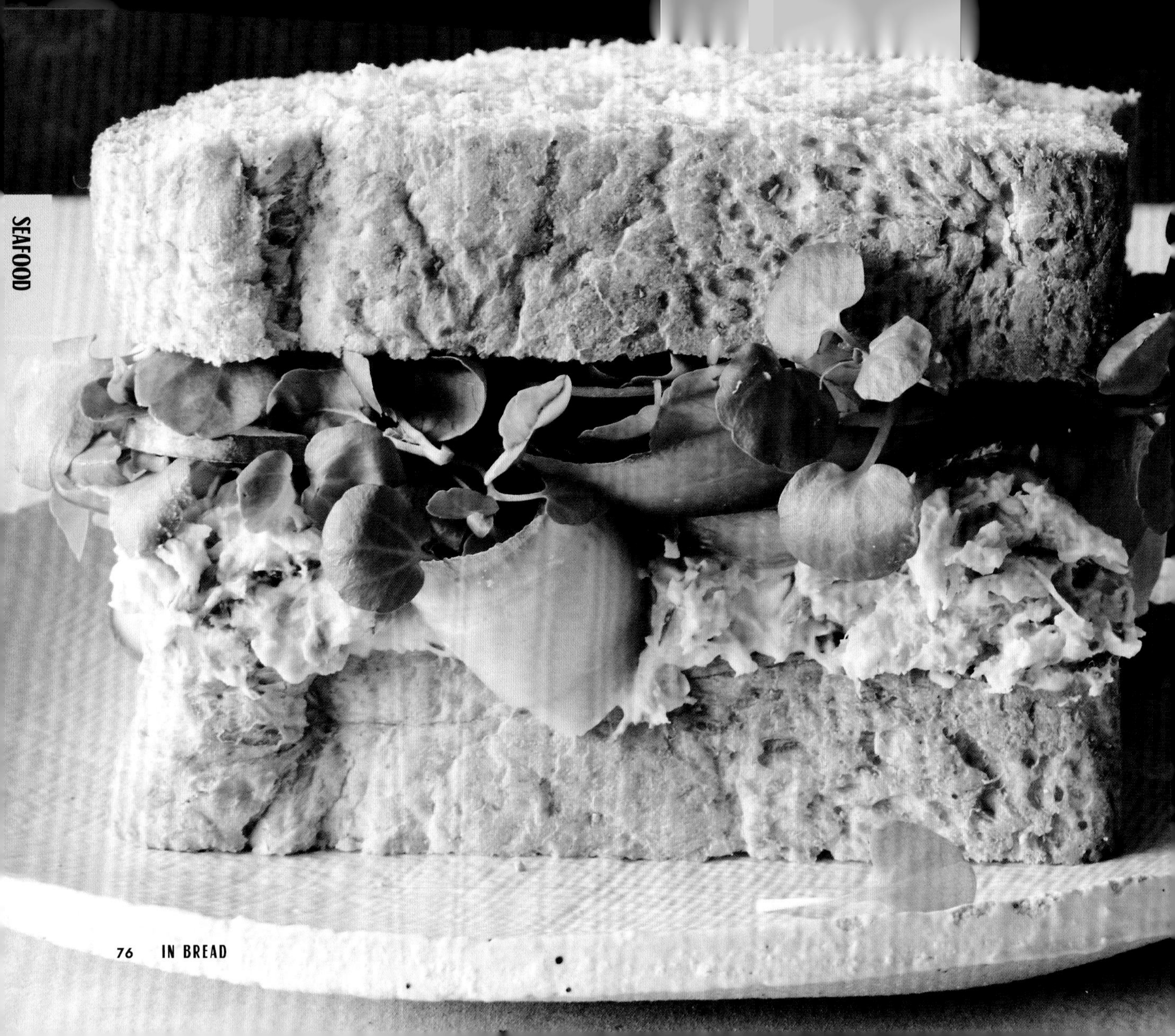

This is a doorstep classic. Summery and fresh, it hits all the right spots in all the right places. Not only is mackerel extremely good for you, it is also one of the few fish that is still considered sustainable. Horseradish and smoked fish make the perfect couple on the culinary dating scene, so it's only natural that we put them together in a sandwich. This is marvellous served with a pint of stout on a summer's afternoon.

SMOKED MACKEREL WITH WATERCRESS

SERVES 2

1 heaped teaspoon grated horseradish

125 g (4½ oz/½ cup) crème fraîche

a few dill fronds

juice of ½ lemon

1 teaspoon capers, rinsed and chopped

200 g (7 oz) smoked mackerel

butter, for spreading

4 slices wholemeal (whole-wheat) bread, cut 2.5 cm (1 in) thick

½ small cucumber, cut into ribbons

¼ red onion, thinly sliced

large handful watercress

1. Combine the horseradish, crème fraîche, dill, lemon juice and capers in a small bowl. Season well with black pepper.

2. Flake the mackerel into the bowl and mix well. Set aside in the fridge for 10 minutes for the flavours to develop.

3. Butter the bread and spoon the mackerel mixture onto 2 slices. Layer the cucumber ribbons on top then add the red onion, watercress and remaining slices of bread.

The good ol' tuna melt – filling up individuals who have nothing in their fridge apart from a small block of suspect-looking cheese, a few vegetable scraps in the crisper and a tin of tuna in the pantry for as long as humans have been putting fish in a tin. Do not underestimate the deliciousness of this end-of-pay-cycle sandwich treat.

THE TUNA MELT

SERVES 2

180 g (6½ oz) tinned tuna

¼ red onion, finely chopped

1 small celery stalk, thinly sliced

2 tablespoons sweetcorn kernels

1 tablespoon whole egg mayonnaise

2 slices white or wholemeal (whole-wheat) bread, cut 2.5 cm (1 in) thick

4 slices jarlsberg cheese or similar

1. Flake the tuna into a small bowl and add the red onion, celery and sweetcorn. Season with a pinch of salt and lots of black pepper, then mix in the mayonnaise.

2. Preheat the grill (broiler) to high. Lightly toast the bread on both sides.

3. Spoon the tuna mixture onto the bread and place the cheese on top. Grill for 2–3 minutes until the cheese is melted and bubbling.

Fish fingers (or fish sticks if you're Stateside) have come a long way since their frozen cousins graced the family table over one hundred years ago. Fresh fish, freshly crumbed and fried is just as good as any battered fish, especially when served in white bread with a kick-ass tartare sauce. The jury is out on the addition of tomato ketchup. I think it's crucial but Ais disagrees. We'll leave you to decide for yourself.

FISH FINGER SANDWICH

vegetable oil, for deep-frying

flour, for dredging

1 egg beaten with
1 tablespoon milk

panko breadcrumbs,
for crumbing

200 g (7 oz) flathead fillets
or any firm white fish

4 slices white bread, cut
2.5 cm (1 in) thick

tomato ketchup (optional)

small handful rocket
(arugula)

TARTARE SAUCE

¼ white onion, finely
chopped

2 tablespoons whole egg
mayonnaise

2 Dill pickles (page 167),
finely chopped

juice of ½ lemon

1 teaspoon dijon mustard

1 tablespoon finely chopped
parsley

1. To make the tartare sauce, place the onion in a small bowl of cold water and set aside for 15 minutes to remove the harshness of the onion flavour. Drain, then combine with the remaining ingredients. Season with salt and pepper to taste and set aside.

2. Heat enough oil for deep-frying to 170°C (340°F) or until a cube of bread dropped into the oil turns brown in 15 seconds.

3. Place the flour, egg and milk, and breadcrumbs in three separate shallow bowls.

4. Cut the fish fillets into fat fingers (we used 2 flathead fillets per sandwich). Working in batches, dredge the fish in the flour, followed by the egg and milk mixture. Thoroughly coat in the breadcrumbs and set aside in the fridge for 10 minutes. If you like your fish fingers to be extra crunchy, double-crumb them by re-dipping in the egg and milk and breadcrumbs.

5. Deep-fry the fish fillets for approximately 4 minutes until golden brown all over. The timing will depend on how fat your fillets are, so watch them carefully to ensure that they don't overcook. Transfer to paper towel to drain.

6. Smear a generous amount of tartare sauce on the bread. Top 2 slices with the fish fingers and squeeze over some tomato ketchup, if using. Pile on the rocket and top with the remaining bread slices.

1 tablespoon plain
(all-purpose) flour

2 eggs beaten with
2 tablespoons milk

100 g (3½ oz) panko breadcrumbs

vegetable oil, for deep-frying

10 tiger prawns, shelled and
deveined

2 long crispy rolls

2 handfuls shredded lettuce

2 Dill pickles (page 167), sliced
lengthways

2 tomatoes, thickly sliced

CREOLE SPICE MIX

1 teaspoon onion powder

1 teaspoon garlic powder

1 teaspoon paprika

½ teaspoon cayenne pepper

½ teaspoon dried oregano

½ teaspoon dried thyme

REMOULADE SAUCE

90 g (3 oz) whole egg mayonnaise

½ teaspoon hot sauce

juice of ½ lemon

1 teaspoon dijon mustard

1 teaspoon grated horseradish

1 teaspoon capers, rinsed

1 spring onion (scallion), thinly

1. To make the remoulade sauce, combine all of the ingredients in a small bowl and season well with black pepper. Set aside in the fridge for 1 hour for the flavours to develop.

2. Meanwhile, combine all of the Creole spice mix ingredients in a shallow bowl. Season well with lots of black pepper. Add the flour and mix well. Place the beaten egg mixed with milk in another shallow bowl and the panko breadcrumbs in a third.

3. Heat enough vegetable oil for deep-frying to 170°C (340°F) or until a cube of bread dropped into the oil turns brown in 15 seconds.

4. Working in batches, dredge the prawns in the spice and flour mix, then dip in the egg and milk and coat in the breadcrumbs. Double-crumb the prawns by re-dunking in the egg and milk and recoating in the breadcrumbs. Your prawns should be completely covered in crisp panko goodness.

5. Deep-fry 3–4 prawns at a time for about 2 minutes on each side until golden brown. Transfer to paper towel to drain.

6. Slice open the top of each roll and spoon in an unhealthy amount of remoulade sauce. Add the shredded lettuce, dill pickle slices and tomato. Shove in the prawns and top with more remoulade sauce.

7. Serve with lots of paper towel… or a bib.

The po'boy, that great New Orleans classic. This very messy, very delicious sandwich has come a long way from humble beginnings to become one of the most popular sandwiches on the *In Bread* scene today. For us, it's all about the remoulade sauce. So tangy and sweet, it goes perfectly with any number of po'boy fillings.

Wait! Don't turn over the page just yet. We promise you that pickled herring is not only delicious it's also really healthy (OK, apart from the butter... and mayonnaise). But seriously, oily fish contains lots of omega 3 goodness, something that most of us don't get enough of. Smørrebrød has been gracing Scandinavian tables for centuries. It's about time the rest of us got on board (or should that be brød?).

PICKLED HERRING ON RYE

SERVES 2

THE CLASSIC
butter, for spreading

2 slices wholegrain rye bread (pumpernickel)

4 pickled herrings, rinsed and cut into bite-sized chunks

juice of ½ lemon

¼ red onion, thinly sliced

a few dill fronds

CURRIED PICKLED HERRING
2 eggs

½ tablespoon whole egg mayonnaise

½ tablespoon sour cream

1 teaspoon capers, rinsed

1 level teaspoon curry powder

1 teaspoon finely chopped dill, plus a few extra fronds, for garnish

4 pickled herrings, rinsed and cut into bite-sized chunks

butter, for spreading

2 slices wholegrain rye bread (pumpernickel)

1. To make a classic pickled herring on rye, generously butter the bread. Combine the pickled herring and lemon juice in a small bowl. Add a pinch of salt and some black pepper.

2. Spoon the herring onto the bread and top with the red onion and a few dill fronds.

3. If you'd like to up the ante with a curried version, place the eggs in a small saucepan and cover with cold water. Bring to the boil then simmer for 5 minutes. Drain and set aside in a bowl of cold water.

4. Combine the mayonnaise, sour cream, capers, curry powder and dill in a small bowl. Season with a pinch of salt and lots of black pepper, then add the pickled herring and mix well.

5. Shell the eggs and cut into thick slices – the yolk should still be slightly runny. Generously butter the bread and spoon on the pickled herring mixture. Top with slices of egg and garnish with the extra dill and a little more black pepper.

PRAWN & MARIE ROSE SAUCE

16 large cooked prawns, shelled and deveined

butter, for spreading

4 slices white or brown bread, cut 2.5 cm (1 in) thick

2 handfuls shredded iceberg lettuce

MARIE ROSE SAUCE

2 tablespoons whole egg mayonnaise

1 tablespoon tomato ketchup

squeeze of lemon juice

1. To make the Marie Rose sauce, combine the ingredients in a small bowl and season well with black pepper. There will be enough salt in the mayo and tomato ketchup without needing to add extra. By all means adjust the quantities here to your liking: lemon juice will add tartness and extra ketchup will make it sweeter.

2. Chop the prawns and add to the sauce, mixing well to combine. Set aside in the fridge for 10 minutes for the flavours to develop.

3. Butter the bread and spoon the prawn mixture on 2 slices of bread. Arrange a handful of lettuce on the prawns and place the remaining bread on top.

Call us children of the '80s, but we love a prawn and Marie Rose sandwich. Remember when prawn cocktails were served in sundae glasses with iceberg lettuce, a squeeze of lemon and a slice of avocado if you were dining somewhere real fancy? Well, here is the sandwich version, except without the avocado, cos sometimes the original is the best.

If you don't happen to live near the Bosphorus then this sandwich is the closest you will get to the ridiculously moreish fish rolls sold along the banks of this mighty river. Freshly grilled fish served with a lemon and caper dressing and plenty of sumac. It takes a warm summer's day to the next level.

BALIK EKMEK
[TURKISH FISH SANDWICH]

2 tablespoons plain (all-purpose) flour

1 × 300 g (10½ oz) firm white fish fillet, cut into 2 equal-sized portions

2 tablespoons chopped parsley leaves

1 tablespoon capers, rinsed

1 garlic clove, finely chopped

juice of 1 lemon

60 ml (2 fl oz/¼ cup) olive oil

2 round crispy rolls, sliced in half

2 teaspoons sumac

¼ red onion, sliced

1 large tomato, thickly sliced

2 large handfuls shredded iceberg lettuce

1. Tip the flour into a shallow bowl and season well with salt and pepper. Dredge the fish fillets in the flour, coating thoroughly. Dust off any excess and set aside.

2. Make a simple dressing by combining the parsley, capers, garlic and lemon juice in a small jar. Season well with salt and pepper, then put the lid on and shake vigorously until well combined.

3. Heat 3 tablespoons of the oil in a heavy-based frying pan over medium–high heat. Add the fish and cook for 5–6 minutes. Flip the fish over and cook for a further 2–3 minutes or until cooked through and flaking in the middle. Remove from the heat and set aside to rest for 5 minutes.

4. Heat a griddle pan over high heat. Drizzle the remaining oil over the cut sides of the bread then place, cut side down, in the pan. Place a plate on top to encourage a few chargrill marks. Once toasted, turn the bread 90° and cook until you have a sexy fishnet-stocking pattern on the insides of your bread.

5. Sprinkle the sumac over the griddled bread and place the fish on the bottom halves. Top with a little of the dressing then add the red onion, tomato and shredded lettuce. Finish with another drizzle of dressing and pop the lids on.

6. Eat immediately. With Prosecco.

If a poll was taken on the most popular sandwich filling, chicken would win, hands (or wings) down. In bread, on bread, underneath bread, chicken sandwiches have been sustaining us ever since the dietary choices of Lord Sandwich caught on. There are so many interpretations using this classic ingredient we could have filled a whole book with chicken sandwiches alone, but that would be slightly unfair, not least on the chicken.

And let's not forget the good old leftover Christmas turkey – the perfect ready-made filling, especially when served with deep-fried brie and cranberry sauce. We've even included a spin on the classic duck pancake, but this time served in brioche. You're welcome!

The turkey club is a souped-up version of a BLT – a triple-decker cut into triangles that harks back to 19th-century America. The toothpick isn't there purely for decoration – it's needed to secure all of the layers into place so that you stand a decent chance of eating it without the whole lot falling apart. Whole egg mayonnaise is a must – there's no room here for the sweet kind.

TURKEY CLUB

SERVES 2

1 teaspoon olive oil

4 slices bacon

6 slices white sandwich bread

whole egg mayonnaise, for spreading

4 large butter lettuce leaves

2 tomatoes, sliced

4 slices turkey

1. Heat the oil in a small frying pan over high heat and fry the bacon until crisp. Set aside and keep warm.

2. Toast the bread.

3. Spread 4 slices of toast with mayonnaise. Top 2 slices with a lettuce leaf followed by the tomato and turkey. Add the remaining toast spread with mayonnaise, then place the bacon on top. Add the remaining lettuce leaves and toast slices, and lightly press down to help everything stick together.

4. Cut into triangles, securing with a toothpick.

If you think the brioche is going to make this delicious treat too sweet, feel free to use any bread of your choosing. However, it does add to the decadence of this sandwich, and the sweetness is offset by the sharpness of the cheese.

PEKING DUCK WITH PICKLED CUCUMBER & CHEDDAR

SERVES 2

2 tablespoons hoisin sauce

4 slices brioche, cut 2.5 cm (1 in) thick

200 g (7 oz) Peking duck (see note), shredded

4 thin slices mature cheddar

1 spring onion (scallion), sliced into matchsticks

pickled cucumber ribbons (see recipe below)

PICKLED CUCUMBER

100 g (3½ oz) sugar

1 tablespoon salt

240 ml (8 fl oz) white vinegar

1 small cucumber, cut into ribbons

1. To make the pickled cucumber, heat the sugar, salt and vinegar in a small saucepan over medium heat. Cook, stirring occasionally, until the sugar is dissolved. Remove from the heat and set aside to cool.

2. Place the cucumber in a sterilised jar and pour over the pickling liquid. Pop the lid on and transfer to the fridge. The pickled cucumber will be good to eat after 4–5 hours, and will keep for up to 1 week in the fridge.

3. To assemble, spread the hoisin sauce on the brioche. Divide the duck between 2 slices, then top with the cheese, spring onion, a few slices of pickled cucumber and the remaining brioche.

Note: You can buy Peking duck from most Asian grocers and some Chinese restaurants. Alternatively, some supermarkets sell them in portions that just need roasting in the oven, resulting in warm duck, which just adds to the yumminess. For this recipe, we used two leg portions, which yielded approximately 230 g (8 oz) of meat, once shredded.

Korean-fried chicken, chicken karaage, Southern-fried chicken –
however you like it best, there are few things more satisfying than
shoving piping hot deep-fried chicken into your gob. Although
6th July, National Fried Chicken Day, is only celebrated in
America, we can all get into the spirit any day of the week with
this ridiculously good sandwich, served with crunchy, spicy
slaw. And not a bucket in sight...

FRIED CHICKEN WITH
SPICY BUTTERMILK SLAW

SERVES 2

4 chicken thigh fillets
vegetable oil, for deep-frying
mayonnaise, for spreading
2 bread rolls, sliced in half

MARINADE
300 ml (10 fl oz) buttermilk
1 tablespoon black pepper
1 teaspoon mustard powder
1 teaspoon cayenne pepper

COATING
250 g (9 oz) plain
(all-purpose) flour
2 tablespoons baking powder
2 tablespoons onion powder
1 tablespoon garlic powder
1 teaspoon salt

SPICY BUTTERMILK SLAW
100 ml (3½ fl oz) buttermilk
2 tablespoons mayonnaise
1 tablespoon sour cream
½ teaspoon cayenne pepper
squeeze of lime juice
1 medium-sized carrot, grated
100 g (3½ oz) red cabbage,
shredded
2 spring onions (scallions),
thinly sliced

1. To make the marinade, combine all of the ingredients in a container or zip lock bag. Add the chicken, and massage the marinade into the chicken until well coated. Set aside in the fridge for a minimum of 2 hours, but preferably overnight.

2. Combine the coating ingredients in a zip lock bag.

3. Heat enough vegetable oil for deep-frying to 180°C (350°F), or until a cube of bread dropped into the oil turns brown in 15 seconds.

4. Working with one piece of chicken at a time, toss in the coating mixture, ensuring that each piece is completely covered. Dip the chicken back in the marinade then coat again in the flour and spices.

5. Working in batches if necessary, carefully transfer the chicken to the hot oil and fry for about 10 minutes, until golden brown and cooked through. Drain on paper towel.

6. Meanwhile, make the slaw. Combine the buttermilk, mayonnaise, sour cream, cayenne pepper and lime juice in a small bowl and whisk until well combined. Season with salt and pepper to taste.

7. Combine the carrot, red cabbage and spring onion in a bowl and toss through the dressing.

8. Spread mayonnaise on the cut sides of each roll then add a large spoonful of slaw followed by the chicken. Top with the remaining roll halves and eat immediately.

Created in honour of the coronation of Queen Elizabeth II in 1953, this sandwich consists of only three basic elements – cooked chicken, curry powder and a creamy sauce. Various incarnations have evolved over the years to include their own special add-ins, from raisins, carrots and almonds to the kitchen sink and old boots (OK, maybe not the last two). Here, we've taken it back to the basics, but with a little extra tang.

CORONATION CHICKEN

SERVES 2

250 g (9 oz) shredded barbecue chicken

butter, for spreading

4 slices multigrain bread, cut 2.5 cm (1 in) thick

2 handfuls watercress or baby spinach leaves

DRESSING

90 g (3 oz) whole egg mayonnaise

2 tablespoons mango chutney

2 teaspoons curry powder

3 teaspoons lemon juice

2 teaspoons dijon mustard

1 teaspoon celery salt

1. To make the dressing, combine all of the ingredients in a bowl and whisk until well combined.

2. Add the chicken and mix well.

3. Generously butter the bread and divide the coronation chicken mixture between 2 slices. Top with a handful of watercress or baby spinach and the remaining bread.

This sweet and oozy cheese sandwich is an excellent way to use up leftovers from the Christmas turkey, especially as Christmas is the one time of year you're likely to actually have cranberry sauce in the house. But, to be honest, it's all about the deep-fried brie here. Make sure you pop the cheese in the fridge to firm up before deep-frying so it doesn't collapse in the hot oil, leaving you with nothing but deep-fried crumbs and a very sad sandwich.

DEEP-FRIED BRIE & TURKEY BAGUETTE

SERVES 2

plain (all-purpose) flour, for dusting

1 egg, beaten

160 g (5½ oz/2 cups) fresh breadcrumbs

200 g (7 oz) firm brie, cut into 8 chunks

80 g (2¾ oz) cranberry sauce

vegetable oil, for deep-frying

handful spinach or other green leaves

2 small baguettes, sliced in half lengthways

4 slices turkey

1. Place the flour, beaten egg and breadcrumbs in three separate shallow bowls.

2. Working with one piece at a time, coat the brie in the flour, then dip in the egg and coat in the breadcrumbs. Set aside in the fridge for 10 minutes to firm up.

3. Place the cranberry sauce and 2 tablespoons water in a small saucepan and heat gently, stirring, until the sauce is a runny consistency.

4. Heat enough oil for deep-frying to 170°C (340°F), or until a cube of bread dropped into the oil turns brown in 15 seconds. Fry the cheese, in batches if necessary, for 1–2 minutes, until golden brown.

5. Divide the green leaves between the baguettes, then pile in the turkey and deep-fried cheese. Spoon the cranberry sauce over the top and season with lots of freshly cracked black pepper.

THERESE'S CHICKEN SCHNITZ

SERVES 2

250 g (9 oz) chicken breast fillet

1 egg

35 g (1¼ oz/¼ cup) plain (all-purpose) flour

50 g (1¾ oz/½ cup) panko breadcrumbs

2 teaspoons paprika

olive oil, for shallow-frying

60 g (2 oz) cheddar, sliced

1 avocado

squeeze of lemon juice

2 crunchy, fluffy bread rolls, cut in half

RAINBOW SLAW

200 g (7 oz) red cabbage, shredded

1 carrot, grated

½ red capsicum (bell pepper), cut into ½ cm (¼ in) dice

½ red onion, thinly sliced

60 g (2 oz) whole egg mayonnaise

1 tablespoon horseradish cream

2 teaspoons lemon juice

1. To make the rainbow slaw, toss together the cabbage, carrot, capsicum and onion in a bowl. In a separate bowl, mix together the mayonnaise, horseradish cream and lemon juice. Add to the vegetable mixture, stir well to combine and set aside.

2. Slice the chicken breast in half lengthways. Pound both pieces with a meat mallet until about ½ cm (¼ in) thick.

3. Lightly whisk the egg in a shallow bowl and season with salt and pepper. Place the flour in a second shallow bowl and the breadcrumbs mixed with the paprika in a third.

4. Dredge each piece of chicken in the flour and shake off the excess. Dip in the egg, then coat well in the breadcrumbs, gently pressing the crumbs into the chicken with your fingertips.

5. Heat 1 cm (½ in) oil in a medium-sized frying pan over medium heat. Cook the chicken for 3–4 minutes on each side until crisp and golden brown. During the final minute of cooking, place the cheese on top of the chicken to melt slightly. Transfer the schnitzels to paper towel to drain.

6. Mash the avocado with the back of a fork, add a squeeze of lemon juice and season with salt and pepper. Spread the avocado on the rolls, then top with the chicken and coleslaw.

7. Hells yeah.

We asked our friend Therese, 'what are your three favourite things?' She replied, 'friends and family, Geelong Football Club and chicken and avocado sandwiches,' in that order. In light of this passion it would be remiss of us not to include Therese's *pièce de résistance*. So here it is, the mighty schnitzel and avocado. Thanks, Tree!

Canada – the land of maple syrup, Mike Myers and the gravy-topped, French-fries wonder that is poutine. Not surprisingly, Canada has another gravy-topped offering – the mighty hot chicken sandwich, which is popular in Quebec. This hot delicious mess consists of bread, chicken, gravy and peas. I, for one, am thankful, O Canada.

HOT CHICKEN SANDWICH

SERVES 2

80 g (2¾ oz/½ cup) frozen peas

butter, for spreading

4 slices white bread, cut 2.5 cm (1 in) thick

240 g (8½ oz) leftover roast chicken, shredded

GRAVY

1 teaspoon butter

1 tablespoon leftover drippings (chicken fat from the roasting pan) (see note)

2 tablespoons plain (all-purpose) flour

1 teaspoon onion powder

½ teaspoon garlic powder

300 ml (10 fl oz) chicken stock

1. To make the gravy, melt the butter and drippings in a small saucepan over low heat. Stir in the flour then cook for 1–2 minutes.

2. Add the onion and garlic powders along with the stock, increase the heat to medium and bring to the boil.

3. Reduce the heat to low and simmer for 5–10 minutes, until nice and thick. Season with salt and pepper to taste.

4. Boil the peas in salted water for 2–3 minutes, then drain and set aside.

5. Butter the bread and arrange the chicken on 2 slices. Place the remaining bread on top and spoon over the gravy and peas.

Note: If you don't have any leftover drippings, you can substitute an extra 1 tablespoon of butter.

CHICKEN GYRO

400 g (14 oz) boneless skinless chicken breasts or thighs

½ tablespoon olive oil

2 Greek pita breads

1 tomato, diced

2–3 thin slices red onion

2 handfuls shredded lettuce

MARINADE

½ teaspoon dried oregano

½ teaspoon smoked paprika

pinch of chilli flakes (optional)

2 tablespoons Greek yoghurt

2 tablespoons lemon juice

2 tablespoons olive oil

TZATZIKI

125 g (4½ oz/½ cup) plain yoghurt

1 garlic clove, crushed

1 teaspoon lemon juice

1 teaspoon finely chopped dill

1 small cucumber

1. To make the marinade, combine the ingredients in a bowl or zip lock bag, along with a pinch of salt and pepper. If using chicken breast, slice it in half lengthways, so that each breast becomes two thinner pieces. Add to the marinade and rub the mixture into the chicken. Set aside in the fridge for 1–2 hours.

2. To make the tzatziki, combine the yoghurt, garlic, lemon juice and dill in a small bowl. Cut the cucumber in half lengthways and scoop out the seeds. Grate the cucumber, then transfer to a few sheets of paper towel or a clean tea towel and roll and twist lighlty to squeeze out the excess moisture. Add the cucumber to the yoghurt mixture, season with salt and pepper to taste and mix well.

3. Preheat the oven to 170°C (340°F).

4. Preheat a barbecue or griddle pan to high and brush with the oil. Drain any excess marinade from the chicken and transfer to the barbecue. Cook the chicken for 5–8 minutes, turning once, until cooked through. Shred the meat using two forks.

5. Warm the pita in the oven for 2–3 minutes. Tear two large squares of baking paper, slightly larger than the pita bread.

6. To assemble, place the pita on the baking paper. Add the tomato, red onion, chicken and lettuce and spoon over several dollops of tzatziki. Tightly roll each gyro in the baking paper and shove it in your mouth immediately.

Derived from the Greek word for 'turning', a gyro is a traditional Greek wrap. Lamb, chicken or beef is seasoned with various herbs and spices, layered onto large spikes and cooked on a rotisserie. The meat is then shaved off and tucked into warm pita bread with salad and tzatziki. This recipe barbecues then shreds the meat, so it is more make-at-home-friendly (as we're guessing you don't have a spit in your kitchen!).

06 /

By virtue of its versatility and deliciousness, there aren't many sandwiches that don't benefit from the addition of a piggy product. Ham (surely, the ultimate sandwich filling?), bacon, sausages or meatballs; fried, grilled, shredded or freshly sliced from the deli – however it comes you know it's going to make you happy.

And then there's the Reuben, perfectly cooked corned beef topped with sauerkraut and pickles or the classic philly cheese steak, a true king in the sandwich world. Whatever you decide to create, make it big and make it delicious.

This delicious sandwich is a popular street food from Hanoi. The bread used, a small crusty baguette, is a remnant of French colonial times. The combination of French (bread and pâté) and Vietnamese (daikon, coriander and chilli) ingredients give this sandwich its unique flavour. It's often made with cold deli-style pork, but we've upped the game with hearty meatballs instead.

PORK MEATBALL BANH MI

SERVES 2

½ quantity Pickled daikon & carrot (page 169)

2 Vietnamese baguettes

mayonnaise, for spreading

pork pâté, for spreading

1 small cucumber, sliced lengthways

½ quantity Pickled daikon & carrot (page 169)

a few coriander (cilantro) leaves

2 birdseye chillies, thinly sliced

Sriracha hot sauce

PORK MEATBALLS

250 g (9 oz) minced (ground) pork

1 garlic clove, finely chopped

1 teaspoon finely chopped ginger

45 g (1½ oz/½ cup) fresh breadcrumbs

1 small egg, lightly beaten

1 teaspoon white pepper

1 tablespoon fish sauce

1 tablespoon finely chopped coriander (cilantro) stalks

1 tablespoon olive oil

1. Start off by making the pork meatballs. Combine all of the ingredients except the olive oil in a bowl and mix well with your hands. Take 2 tablespoons of the mixture and roll it into a ball. Set aside and repeat with the remaining mixture – you should have 8 meatballs.

2. Heat the oil in a frying pan over medium heat and fry the meatballs, in batches if necessary, for 10–15 minutes, until browned all over and cooked through.

3. Slice open the baguettes, but do not cut all the way through. Spread mayonnaise on one side and pâtè on the other. Add the cucumber, pickled daikon and carrot and meatballs.

4. Finish each baguette with a few coriander leaves and as much fresh chilli and hot sauce as you can handle.

MEAT

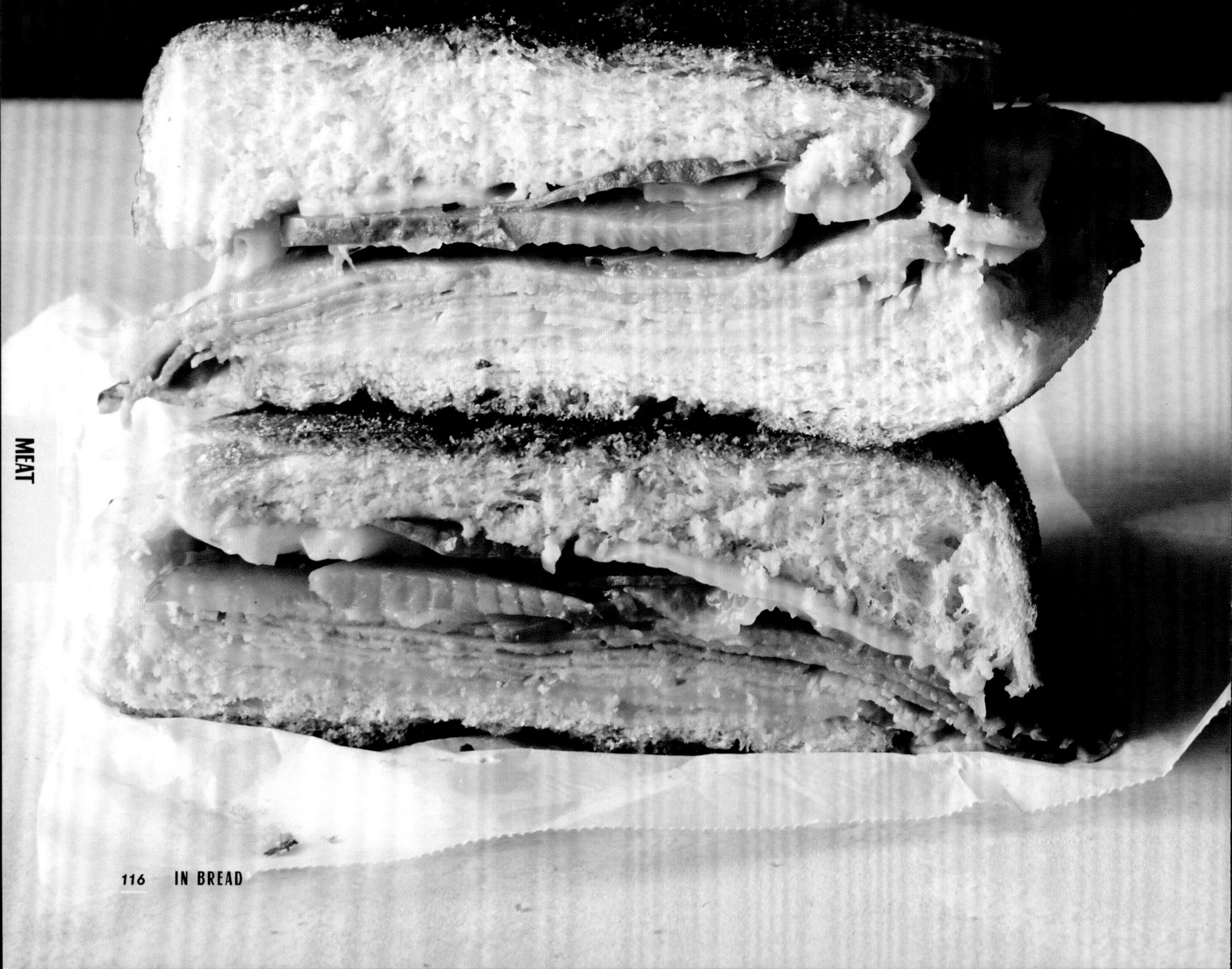

The burning question about this sandwich seems to be: do you have it Miami-style, as in this recipe, or Tampa-style, by adding a few slices of hot salami? Whichever way you go, your sandwich must be cooked on a flat sandwich press, squeezed shut to encourage melty goodness.

THE CUBAN

SERVES 2

2 Cuban bread rolls or long white crusty bread rolls, sliced in half

knob of butter, melted

American mustard, for spreading

4 slices Swiss cheese

6 slices deli roast pork, thinly sliced

4 slices ham, thinly sliced

3 Dill pickles (page 167), thinly sliced

1. Preheat a sandwich press.

2. Place the bottom halves of the rolls, cut side down, on the sandwich press. Brush the outside of each half with melted butter, then flip over and spread the insides with a generous layer of mustard.

3. Place one slice of cheese on the mustard, then add the pork, ham and pickle. Top with the remaining cheese and bread and brush with more melted butter.

4. Close the sandwich press, squeezing down so that the sandwich is compressed. Toast for about 5 minutes, until golden brown and slightly crisp at the edges.

The word 'butty' is a British word for a sandwich, from the words 'buttered bread'. Although many things can be chucked between two slices to make a decent butty, nothing quite beats this classic offering. However you fill yours, there are three rules you must not break: it has to be fresh white bread, it has to be buttered and it has to have lashings of sauce.

BACON & CHIP BUTTY

SERVES 2

2 medium-sized potatoes, cut into batons

vegetable oil, for frying

4 slices bacon

butter, for spreading

4 slices white bread, cut 2.5 cm (1 in) thick

brown sauce or tomato ketchup

1. Rinse the potato in cold water to remove some of the starch. Transfer to a medium-sized saucepan and cover with cold water. Bring to the boil and simmer for 3–4 minutes until parboiled. Drain and gently pat dry with paper towel.

2. Preheat the oven to 220°C (430°F). Pour 3 tablespoons of oil into a roasting tray large enough to hold the potato in a single layer, then transfer to the oven to heat up for 3–4 minutes.

3. Carefully remove the tray from the oven and add the potato, tossing gently in the hot oil until well coated. Return to the oven and cook for 20–25 minutes, turning occasionally, until golden brown.

4. About 5 minutes before your chips are ready, heat 1 teaspoon of oil in a frying pan over medium heat and add the bacon. Cook until crisp or cooked to your liking.

5. Drain the chips on paper towel and season well with salt.

6. Butter the bread and divide the bacon and chips between the sandwiches. Top with brown sauce or tomato ketchup, or both.

Cooked low and slow, pulled pork has long been a staple in many an American barbecue joint. In recent years, its popularity has exploded and it can now be found filling sandwiches from Hackney to Hong Kong. The barbecue sauce in this recipe is super simple to make and can be used for any occasion that calls for a sweet and smoky condiment. Go on, spread the love.

PULLED PORK & SLAW WITH BARBECUE SAUCE

SERVES 6

1 boneless pork shoulder (about 1.5 kg/3 lb 5 oz), skin removed

2 onions, chopped

2 garlic cloves, finely chopped

185 ml (6 fl oz/¾ cup) apple cider vinegar

1 teaspoon hot English mustard

2 tablespoons Worcestershire sauce

2 tablespoons sugar

250 ml (8½ fl oz/1 cup) beer

1 quantity Barbecue sauce (page 173)

1½ quantities Coleslaw (page 172)

6 white bread rolls, sliced in half

DRY RUB

55 g (2 oz/¼ cup) brown sugar

1 teaspoon chilli powder

1 teaspoon smoked paprika

1 teaspoon cayenne pepper

1 teaspoon ground cumin

1. To make the dry rub, combine the ingredients in a bowl. Massage the mixture into the pork shoulder, getting it into all of the creases. Season well with salt, then cover and set aside in the fridge for 2–3 hours, or preferably overnight.

2. Transfer the marinated pork to a large slow cooker. Combine the onion, garlic, apple cider vinegar, mustard, Worcestershire sauce, sugar, beer and 250 g (9 oz) of the barbecue sauce in a bowl and season well with salt and black pepper. Pour the mixture over the pork, pop the lid on and leave to cook on medium heat for 8 hours, turning once or twice to ensure even cooking.

3. Transfer the pork to a large bowl and shred the meat using two forks. Strain the leftover liquid to remove any solids, then return the meat and the juices to the slow cooker until ready to serve.

4. Spoon a large helping of coleslaw onto the bottom half of each roll and pile on the pulled pork. Drizzle over the remaining barbecue sauce and serve immediately.

MAC & CHEESE WITH JALAPEÑOS & BACON

100 g (3 ½ oz) cooked macaroni

1 teaspoon vegetable oil

4 slices bacon

butter, for spreading

4 slices white bread, cut 2.5 cm (1 in) thick

2 tablespoons pickled jalapeños

hot sauce, to serve

BÉCHAMEL SAUCE

15 g (½ oz) butter

15 g (½ oz) plain (all-purpose) flour

250 ml (8½ fl oz/1 cup) milk

70 g (2½ oz) red Leicester cheese, grated

30 g (1 oz) mature cheddar, grated

1 teaspoon seeded mustard

1. To make the béchamel sauce, melt the butter in a small saucepan over medium heat until foaming. Add the flour, and cook, stirring frequently, for 1–2 minutes. Add the milk and whisk constantly for 5–10 minutes until you have a thick and smooth sauce. Bring to the boil and add the cheese, then turn off the heat and continue to stir until the cheese is melted. Stir in the mustard, the cooked macaroni and season to taste.

2. Heat the oil in a frying pan over medium heat and add the bacon. Cook until crisp or cooked to your liking.

3. Heat a large frying pan over medium heat. Butter the bread and place 2 slices, butter side down, in the pan. Pile the macaroni cheese onto the bread, then top with jalapeños and bacon.

4. Place the remaining bread, butter side up, on top and fry for 2–3 minutes on both sides until nice and golden brown.

5. Serve with your favourite hot sauce on the side.

MEAT

Mac and cheese is one of the ultimate comfort foods; all that creamy goodness is guaranteed to make you feel content. This recipe makes a feast of any leftover cheesy pasta you have lying around, although this sandwich is so good in its own right, it's worth making from scratch. Just omit the bacon for a veggie version.

The size of this sandwich may appear comical, and that's because it is. Ba-da-boom! 1930s comic-book character Dagwood Bumstead was often depicted constructing massive deli meat, cheese and salad sandwiches. It became so well known that it is now part of the American culinary vernacular.

THE DAGWOOD

SERVES 2

mayonnaise, for spreading

4 slices wholemeal (whole-wheat) sandwich bread

8 butter lettuce leaves

4 slices hot sopressa

2 slices emmental

¼ small red onion, thinly sliced

4 slices white sandwich bread

American mustard, for spreading

6 slices beef pastrami

2 Dill pickles (page 167), sliced lengthways

2 slices provolone

2 slices honey-glazed ham

1 tomato, thinly sliced

2 slices turkey

2 slices pepper jack cheese, or similar

1. Spread a generous layer of mayonnaise on the wholemeal bread. Place 2 lettuce leaves, the hot sopressa, emmental and red onion on 2 slices.

2. Spread 2 white slices of bread with mustard and place on top of the red onion with the mustard facing upwards. Add the pastrami, pickle, provolone and ham. Top with the remaining wholemeal bread with the mayonnaise facing upwards.

3. Place the remaining lettuce leaves on top then add the tomato, turkey and pepper jack cheese. Spread the remaining 2 white slices with mustard and place on top.

4. Potentially dislocate jaw to consume.

When you make this sandwich, you will discover that it's a labour of love (albeit a new-found love). Take the time to slice the beef wafer-thin – the end result (we promise) is so worth it. Chuck the steak in the freezer for a few minutes before slicing to help firm it up.

STEAK & MUSHROOM

SERVES 2

olive oil, for frying

200 g (7 oz) beef steak, very thinly sliced

1 large onion, sliced

1 large red capsicum (bell pepper), thinly sliced

200 g (7 oz) cup mushrooms, thinly sliced

whole egg mayonnaise, for spreading

2 baguettes, sliced lengthways

1. Heat a splash of olive oil in a large saucepan over high heat. Add the steak and fry for 2–3 minutes, until just cooked through. Remove from the pan and set aside.

2. Reduce the heat to medium and add another splash of oil to the pan. Add the onion, capsicum and mushrooms and cook, stirring frequently, for 10–15 minutes until soft – the vegetables should be almost silky and not browned.

3. Return the steak to the pan and season well with salt and lots of black pepper. Cover, and cook gently for about 20 minutes, stirring from time to time to prevent the mixture sticking to the bottom of the pan. The mixture should be wet, so add a few splashes of water to the pan if it begins to look too dry.

4. Slather mayonnaise into the baguettes and spoon in the filling. The juice will go everywhere, so heavy-duty napkins are definitely recommended. You have been warned!

Bocadillos are found all over Spain, often served as tapas in bars and restaurants. Their deliciousness lies in their simplicity – rustic-style bread filled with only one or two quality ingredients. Fillings vary from region to region, but staples include multiple styles of chorizo, omelette (tortilla), tuna, cheese and ham.

CHORIZO & PROSCIUTTO BOCADILLOS

SERVES 2

CHORIZO BOCADILLO

1 semi-soft chorizo

1 teaspoon olive oil

1 long crusty bread roll or mini rustic baguette, sliced in half

PROSCIUTTO BOCADILLO

1 long crusty bread roll or mini rustic baguette, sliced in half

½ tomato

olive oil, for drizzling

3 slices prosciutto

3 slices manchego cheese

1. To make the chorizo bocadillo, cut the chorizo into long rounds.

2. Heat the olive oil in a frying pan over medium–high heat. Fry the chorizo until the fat oozes out and melts, about 3–4 minutes, then remove the slices from the pan and set aside. Leave the oil in the pan, which will now be a nice orange-red colour.

3. Reduce the heat to medium. Place the roll or baguette, cut side down, into the pan and cook for 1–2 minutes to soak up the oil. Transfer to a plate and place the chorizo in the bread.

4. To make the prosciutto bocadillo, rub each cut side of the bread roll or baguette with the cut side of the tomato, pressing it into the bread so it absorbs some of the flavour.

5. Drizzle with olive oil and alternate the prosciutto and cheese on top.

Corned beef is a salt-cured beef. The 'corn' refers to the large rocks or 'corns' of salt used to cure the meat (as opposed to the yellow foodstuff). Here, we've paired it with a sweet mustard pickle, a twist on the classic mustard and corned beef combo.

CORNED BEEF BAGEL WITH SWEET MUSTARD PICKLE

SERVES 2

2 poppy seed bagels, sliced in half

60 g (2 oz) sweet mustard pickle

2 handfuls watercress

CORNED BEEF

1 × 600 g (1 lb 5 oz) piece corned silverside (beef brisket)

1 onion, quartered

125 ml (4 fl oz/½ cup) white vinegar

10 whole cloves

10 black peppercorns

2–3 dried bay leaves

1 tablespoon brown sugar

1. To make the corned beef, place the beef in a large saucepan, add the remaining ingredients and cover with cold water. Bring to the boil, pop the lid on and simmer for 2 hours. Remove from the heat and set aside to cool.

2. Slice the beef into thinnish slices – you will need about 120 g (4½ oz) beef per bagel. The leftover beef will keep in the fridge for 2–3 days.

3. Spread the bottom half of each bagel with sweet pickle, then top with the beef and a handful of watercress.

As the name suggests, Boston baked beans originated in Boston, although they were often made using molasses instead of maple syrup, which is more commonly used today. The beans were cooked in large earthenware pots that would keep the beans warm overnight and throughout the next day.

BOSTON BAKED BEAN & CHEDDAR JAFFLE

SERVES 2

butter, for spreading

four slices wholemeal (wholewheat) bread

60 g (2 oz) cheddar cheese, grated

BOSTON BAKED BEANS

1 smoked ham hock, or the leftover bone from a Christmas ham (you will need about 100 g/3½ oz meat)

75 g (2¾ oz) dried borlotti beans soaked in cold water overnight

75 g (2¾ oz) cannellini beans, soaked in cold water overnight

1 tablespoon olive oil

½ onion, chopped

2 tablespoons maple syrup

400 g (14 oz) tin diced tomatoes

2 tablespoons Worcestershire sauce

1 tablespoon tomato ketchup

2 tablespoons dijon mustard

1. To make the Boston baked beans, remove any skin and visible fat from the ham.

2. Drain the beans and transfer to a heavy-based oven-proof saucepan with a lid. Add the ham hock or bone and cover with cold water. Bring to the boil, then reduce the heat and simmer for 20 minutes. Drain the beans and the hock, reserving the cooking water.

3. Remove the meat from the hock and dice into small pieces. Preheat the oven to 180°C (350°F).

4. Return the pan to medium heat and add the olive oil. Add the onion and gently cook until soft and translucent. Stir in the maple syrup, tomatoes, Worcestershire sauce, tomato ketchup and dijon mustard. Return the beans and the chopped ham to the pan, along with 250 ml (8½ fl oz/1 cup) of the reserved cooking liquid. Stir well to combine.

5. Pop the lid on the saucepan and transfer to the bottom shelf of the oven. Cook for 1–1½ hours, checking occasionally and adding more cooking liquid if the mixture looks like it's drying out. Season to taste.

6. Heat a jaffle maker and butter one side of the bread. Heap 2 tablespoons of beans and a handful of grated cheese onto the unbuttered side of 2 slices. Top with the remaining bread, butter side up, and transfer to the jaffle maker. Toast until nice and brown or cooked to your liking.

The torta is Mexico's mighty sandwich. And what a sandwich it is. Served hot or cold, ingredients vary, but the staples include refried beans, meat, avocado and salad, all smashed into a roll. If your torta looks too huge to be consumed by a human mouth, then you know you've got your proportions right. Keep the napkins handy for inevitable spillages.

THE TORTA

SERVES 2

60 g (2 oz) refried beans

1 teaspoon olive oil

2 frankfurters, sliced into rounds

2 eggs, lightly beaten

2 white bread rolls, sliced in half

6 slices hot salami

4 slices provolone

1 avocado, sliced

1 large tomato, sliced

½ small white onion, sliced

2 tablespoons pickled jalapeños

1. Heat the beans in a small saucepan over low heat until piping hot. Set aside.

2. Heat the oil in a small frying pan over high heat and add half of the frankfurter. Fry for 1–2 minutes, flipping occasionally, until they are heated through and starting to crisp. Reduce the heat to medium then pour in half of the beaten egg. Fry gently, turning once, until the egg is cooked through and you have a little frankfurter-egg pancake. Repeat with the remaining frankfurter and beaten egg.

3. Heat a grill (broiler) to high. Toast the cut sides of the bread rolls.

4. Spread the bottom half of each roll with the refried beans. Top with the salami, frankfurter-and-egg pancake, provolone, avocado, tomato, onion and jalapeños.

5. Place the bread roll lids on top and press down so that all of the ingredients squish together.

Corned beef, lashings of Russian dressing, sauerkraut and Swiss cheese are the makings of this classic sandwich, created in America as early as the 1910s. Some claim it was created in the famous New York deli Reuben's, while others swear it was born in Omaha, Nebraska, as a snack for a participant in a late-night poker game. Wherever it came from this sandwich is legendary.

THE REUBEN

SERVES 2

4 slices wholemeal (whole-wheat) rye bread

melted butter, for spreading

4 slices Swiss cheese

300 g (10½ oz) corned beef (see recipe on page 130), cut into very thin slices

80 g (2¾ oz) sauerkraut

Dill pickles (page 167), to serve (optional)

RUSSIAN DRESSING

150 g (5½ oz) whole egg mayonnaise

3 tablespoons tomato ketchup

1 tablespoon grated horseradish

60 g (2 oz) cornichons, finely chopped

¼ small white onion, very finely chopped

1. To make the Russian dressing, mix all of the ingredients in a bowl. Season with salt and pepper to taste and set aside.

2. Brush one side of the bread with the melted butter and place 2 slices in a frying pan over medium heat, butter side down. Place a slice of cheese on top, followed by the corned beef and sauerkraut. Spoon over the dressing, then add the remaining cheese and bread, butter side up.

3. Toast for 2–3 minutes then with your finest dexterity, flip the sandwich over and toast the other side until the cheese begins to melt.

4. Serve with dill pickles, if using (we really do recommend this, we just forgot to put them in the shot!).

Depending on where in America you order this iconic sandwich it may be called a hero (New York City), a po'boy (New Orleans), a hoagie (Philadelphia) or a sub (just about everywhere else). However you order it, you will most likely be served an extremely huge sandwich (foot-long? Yes please!).

MEATBALL SUB

SERVES 2

1½ tablespoons olive oil

2 large garlic cloves, thinly sliced

400 g (14 oz) tin crushed tomatoes

6–7 basil leaves, thinly sliced

pinch of dried oregano

2 long soft sesame bread rolls, sliced open

4 slices provolone

MEATBALLS

150 g (5½ oz) minced (ground) beef

150 g (5½ oz) minced (ground) pork

1 garlic clove, finely chopped

1 teaspoon dried oregano

½ medium-sized white onion, finely chopped

¼ teaspoon cayenne pepper

50 g (1¾ oz/½ cup) finely grated parmesan

1 small egg, beaten

1. To make the meatballs, mix all of the ingredients except the egg in a large bowl. Slowly add the beaten egg to bind the mixture (you may not need all of it – too much liquid leads to a soggy meatball). Shape the mixture into 8 balls.

2. Heat ½ tablespoon of the olive oil in a medium-sized frying pan over medium heat and add the garlic. Fry for a few seconds until just starting to brown, then add the tomatoes, basil, oregano and 250 ml (8½ fl oz/1 cup) water. Season to taste and stir well to combine. Bring to the boil, then reduce the heat to low and simmer for about 30 minutes, stirring occasionally, until reduced and thick.

3. Heat the remaining oil in a frying pan over medium heat and fry the meatballs, turning often, for 10–15 minutes, until cooked through.

4. Preheat the grill (broiler) to high.

5. Place the bread rolls on a foil-covered baking tray. Shove 4 meatballs into each roll then cover with 1–2 large tablespoons of the tomato sauce. Place the cheese on top and grill for 3–4 minutes, until the cheese is melted.

As famous as France is for its baguettes, it's the croque that's the king of French sandwiches. If you can't spring for the flight to sample its goodness while sitting outside a Parisian bistro, fear not – this fancy version of a ham and cheese toastie is super easy to make at home. The béchamel needs to be quite thick to ensure that the bread doesn't go soggy.

CROQUE MONSIEUR

SERVES 2

4 slices white bread, cut 2.5 cm (1 in) thick
dijon mustard, for spreading
4 slices good-quality ham
50 g (1¾ oz) gruyère, grated
Dill pickles (page 167) or cornichons, to serve

BÉCHAMEL SAUCE
15 g (½ oz) butter
15 g (½ oz) plain (all-purpose) flour
50 g (1¾ oz) gruyère, grated
1 teaspoon wholegrain (seeded) mustard
250 ml (8½ fl oz/1 cup) full-cream (whole) milk

1. Preheat the grill (broiler) to high.

2. To make the béchamel sauce, melt the butter in a small saucepan over medium heat until foaming. Add the flour, and cook, stirring frequently, for 1–2 minutes. Add the milk and whisk constantly for 5–10 minutes until you have a thick and smooth sauce. Bring to the boil and add the gruyère and mustard, then turn off the heat and continue to stir until the cheese is melted. Season to taste and set aside.

3. Toast the bread on one side under the grill. Spread dijon mustard on the untoasted side of each slice then transfer 2 slices, toasted side down, to a baking sheet or heatproof frying pan. Add the ham, then the gruyère and pop the slices under the grill for a few moments to melt.

4. Place the remaining 2 slices of bread on top, toasted side up. It's a good idea to gently press down to compress the sandwich at this point, so that you have a level top slice to prevent the béchamel sauce from sliding off.

5. Spoon a ladleful of sauce over each sandwich, then return to the grill and cook until the béchamel is bubbling.

6. Serve immediately with dill pickles or cornichons, and a green salad on the side if you're feeling guilty about all the cheese you're about to eat.

Legend goes that hotdog-stand vendor Pat Olivieri created Philadelphia's most famous sandwich in 1930, selling it first to taxi drivers and then to the masses. Although this sandwich is often made with Cheese Whiz (aka cheese from a can), here we've opted for provolone, a common and slightly more sophisticated substitute. When in Philly, an order of a 'one provolone with', should get you a sandwich just like this one.

PHILLY CHEESE STEAK

SERVES 2

2 tablespoons olive oil

2 small white onions, sliced

1 small green capsicum (bell pepper), thinly sliced

400 g (14 oz) steak, thinly sliced into strips

6 slices provolone

2 long soft bread rolls, sliced open

1. Heat the oil in a large frying pan over medium–high heat. Add the onion and capsicum and cook, stirring frequently, until the vegetables begin to char.

2. Remove from the pan and set aside in a bowl. Increase the heat to high and add the steak. Cook for 2–3 minutes until well browned and cooked through.

3. Return the onion and capsicum to the pan and stir to combine. Separate the mixture into two piles approximately the same shape as your bread rolls.

4. Reduce the heat and divide the provolone between the two piles. Cook until the cheese has partially melted then, using a large spatula (or perhaps two), transfer the steak and onion mixtures to the rolls. Press the sandwich together and consume immediately.

MEAT

As with the Greek gyro (see page 108), the shawarma is named after the Arabic word for 'turning' – the manner in which the meat is traditionally cooked, rotating on a spit. Both are said to have originated from the Turkish doner kebab, usually consisting of meat and salad, wrapped in a flatbread or pita. This is our cheat's version.

LAMB SHAWARMA

SERVES 2

250 g (9 oz) diced lamb

1 tablespoon olive oil

2 large Lebanese flatbreads

2 tablespoons hummus

2 handfuls shredded iceberg lettuce

1 large tomato, sliced

2–3 thin slices onion

a few Pickled turnips (page 168)

2 tablespoons Tahini sauce (page 173)

SHAWARMA MARINADE

½ teaspoon paprika

½ teaspoon cracked black pepper

½ teaspoon salt

½ teaspoon ground allspice

¼ teaspoon ground cardamom

60 g (2 oz/¼ cup) natural yoghurt

1 tablespoon olive oil

1 tablespoon lemon juice

small handful chopped coriander (cilantro)

1. To make the marinade, combine all of the ingredients in a bowl. Add the lamb and massage the marinade into the meat. Cover and set aside in the fridge to marinate for 3–4 hours, or preferably overnight.

2. Heat the oil in a large frying pan over high heat. Shake the excess marinade off the lamb and add the meat to the pan. Cook, stirring frequently, for 3–5 minutes until cooked through. Discard the leftover marinade.

3. Preheat a sandwich press.

4. Cut two squares of aluminium foil that are slightly bigger than your flatbreads. Place the flatbreads on the foil and spread the hummus on the bread. Top with the lettuce, tomato, lamb, onion and pickled turnips. Drizzle over the tahini sauce.

5. Using the foil to assist you, tightly roll up the flatbreads, enclosing the filling as you roll. Twist the foil ends and transfer the shawarmas to the sandwich press.

6. Toast for 3–4 minutes until heated through, then slice the shawarmas in half, peel back the foil and enjoy.

If you're fortunate enough to have any leftovers from a delicious roast beef dinner, pairing the cold meat with slices of vinegary beetroot is a good way to avoid feeling like you're eating yesterday's dinner today. Lashings of creamy goat's cheese adds bite and peppery rocket (arugula) rounds out the flavour.

BEEF, BEETROOT & GOAT'S CHEESE

SERVES 2

100 g (3½ oz) soft goat's cheese

4 slices multigrain bread

240 g (8½ oz) leftover roast beef, thinly sliced, or deli roast beef

4 slices Pickled beetroot (page 168)

2 handfuls rocket (arugula)

1. Spread the goat's cheese evenly on the bread.

2. Place the beef on 2 slices and top with the beetroot.

3. Finish with a handful of rocket and the remaining bread.

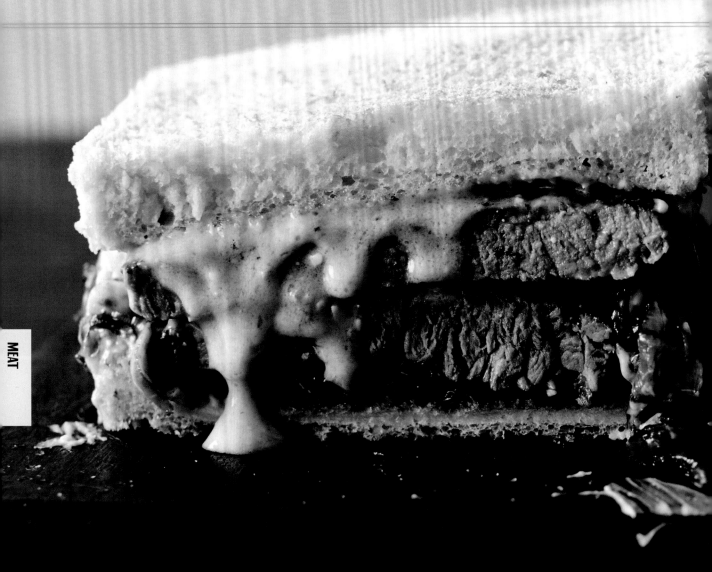

Quick-fried steak, sharp blue cheese and sweet, sweet onions are a match made in heaven. If you don't use all of the blue cheese sauce in the sandwich, we suggest you keep the extra on the side to dip the sandwich into as you eat. It also makes an excellent dipping sauce for chicken wings. Any leftover caramelised onions will keep for 3–4 days in the fridge.

STEAK SANDWICH WITH BLUE CHEESE & CARAMELISED ONIONS

SERVES 2

1 teaspoon olive oil

2 pieces (about 150 g/5½ oz each) thin frying steak

4 slices white sandwich bread

BLUE CHEESE SAUCE

100 g (3½ oz) soft blue cheese

2 tablespoons sour cream

1 tablespoon whole egg mayonnaise

1 garlic clove, crushed

CARAMELISED ONIONS

2 tablespoons olive oil

2 medium-sized onions, thinly sliced

1 tablespoon balsamic vinegar

1 tablespoon sugar

1. To make the blue cheese sauce, mix all of the ingredients in the small bowl of a food processor until smooth.

2. To make the caramelised onions, heat the oil in a heavy-based saucepan over medium heat. Add the onion and cook for 15–20 minutes, stirring frequently to prevent the onion sticking to the base of the pan and adding a little water if the mixture becomes too dry. Add the vinegar and sugar, and stir well to combine. Continue cooking until the onion is dark brown and caramelised.

3. Heat the olive oil in a frying pan over high heat. Add the steak and fry for 2–3 minutes on each side, until just cooked through.

4. Toast the bread.

5. Place the steak on 2 slices of bread and pile the onion on top. Spoon over lashings of blue cheese sauce and top with the remaining bread.

From the ridiculous to the sublime, these sweet sandwiches are guaranteed to make you popular. Whip up some of these babies and you'll have a talking point until it's time for everyone to go home, although you might have to skip dinner to actually fit them in. Or if you're not in the mood to share, you can keep them all to yourself. Who are we to judge how many doughnut bagels you eat?

When creating the recipes for this book, we struggled to come up with a dessert option encased in bread. And then we remembered the brilliant summer pudding – tons of bready goodness soaked in delicious fruit syrup, enclosing fresh summer berries. We've taken it up a notch by adding layers of lemon mascarpone in between the fruit, which, when cut open, gives the pudding the full sandwich effect.

SUMMER PUDDING SANDWICH

SERVES 4

350 g (12½ oz) fresh or frozen blackberries

250 g (9 oz) fresh raspberries

400 g (14 oz) fresh strawberries, hulled and roughly chopped

3 tablespoons lemon juice

60 g (2 oz) caster (superfine) sugar

250 g (9 oz) mascarpone

zest of 2 lemons

2 tablespoons icing (confectioners') sugar

14–20 slices white sandwich bread, crusts removed

1. Place the blackberries, raspberries and strawberries in three separate saucepans. Add 1 tablespoon lemon juice to each pan. Add 1 tablespoon caster sugar to the blackberries and 1 tablespoon to the strawberries. Tip the remaining sugar into the raspberries.

2. Heat all three saucepans over medium heat for about 5 minutes, until the sugar is dissolved and the fruit is just starting to break down. Remove from the heat and strain the liquid from all three pans into a heatproof bowl. Set aside in the fridge to cool.

3. Combine the mascarpone, lemon zest and icing sugar in a small bowl and set aside in the fridge to firm up.

4. Line a 1.5 litre (51 fl oz/6 cup) capacity pudding bowl with two layers of plastic wrap with overhanging ends.

5. Tear the corners off one bread slice. Slice the remaining bread slices in half. Dip the torn bread slice into the cooled fruit syrup and place in the bottom of the bowl. Continue to dip the bread into the syrup and gradually line the bowl with vertical bread slices until you reach the top. You should still have some undipped bread left.

6. Spoon the raspberries into the bowl and cover with undipped bread slices. Spread over half the mascarpone and top with more bread. Add the strawberries and repeat this process, finishing with the blackberries on top. You will probably need to squash down the filling to fit it all in. Dip the remaining bread into the syrup and cover the blackberries, making sure there are no holes at the edge. Wrap the overhanging plastic wrap over the pudding and place a plate and two tins on top to help weigh it down. Transfer to the fridge and chill overnight.

7. Slice the summer pudding into quarters and serve.

Legend has it that Elvis Presley, The King himself, had a fondness for this tasty banana, bacon and peanut butter fried sandwich, so much so that it's become synonymous with his name. Warning: the maple bacon recipe, once tried, can be highly addictive, so you may want to make double the amount to ensure that at least a few slices actually make it into your sandwich. As for the peanut butter – crunchy or smooth, that's up to you to decide, little darlin'.

FRIED ELVIS WITH MAPLE BACON

SERVES 2

4 slices bacon

2 tablespoons maple syrup, plus extra to serve (optional)

80 g (2¾ oz) peanut butter

4 slices white or wholemeal (whole-wheat) sandwich bread

2 bananas, thinly sliced

knob of butter

1. Preheat the oven to 180°C (350°F). Place the bacon on a wire rack over a roasting tin, then roast for 15 minutes, until browned but not crisp.

2. Carefully remove from the oven and brush the bacon all over with the maple syrup, ensuring that each side is well coated. Return to the oven for 5 minutes, then set aside to cool.

3. To assemble, spread 1 tablespoon of peanut butter on each slice of bread. Top 2 slices with the banana and the other 2 slices with bacon, then shmush the two halves together.

4. Melt the butter in a non-stick frying pan over medium heat.

5. Add the sandwiches and fry for 3–4 minutes on each side, until golden brown.

6. Drizzle with maple syrup if using, and serve immediately, remembering that the contents will be super hot!

If there is one absolutely ridiculous recipe in this book, this is it. Yep, who knows what we were thinking when we came up with this gem of a sandwich. But actually, it turns out we were on to something stupidly brilliant. A bagel is round, a doughnut is round, why not put the two together? Especially when you also squirt your own tower of cream on top. The challenge is to eat it without licking your lips.

DOUGHNUT BAGEL WITH WHIPPED CREAM & BERRY COMPOTE

SERVES 2

2 large sesame seed bagels, sliced in half

1 large sugar-ring doughnut, sliced in half horizontally

whipped cream (the fake sort from a can)

COMPOTE
400 g (14 oz) fresh or frozen mixed berries

2 tablespoons caster (superfine) sugar

juice of ½ lemon

1. To make the compote, combine all of the ingredients in a small saucepan over medium heat. Bring to the boil and simmer until completely reduced and almost sticking to the pan. This may take up to 20 minutes, but you'll be rewarded with tangy but sweet jammy goodness at the end. Transfer to a heat-proof bowl and set aside in the fridge for a few minutes to cool a little.

2. Lightly toast the bagels and spread a thick layer of warm compote onto each cut half. Place a doughnut half on top of the compote and squirt a generous amount of cream over the top (then upend the can and squirt an even more generous amount into your mouth, remembering the '80s…). Top with the remaining bagel halves and eat immediately.

3. We have no advice for how to eat this sandwich. Good luck.

DULCE DE LECHE GRILLED PINEAPPLE

SERVES 2

1 × 400 ml (14 fl oz) tin condensed milk

zest of ½ lime

¼ teaspoon chilli flakes

knob of butter

2 tablespoons Cointreau

2 tablespoons brown sugar

2 slices fresh pineapple, cut 2 cm (¾ in) thick and cored

2 slices brioche, sliced 2.5 cm (1 in) thick

2 tablespoons flaked coconut, toasted

1. To make the dulce de leche, soak the tin of condensed milk in warm water and remove the label. Transfer to a large saucepan and cover with plenty of cold water. Bring to the boil then simmer for 3 hours, keeping the pan topped up with water to ensure that the tin is always covered (this is the cooking version of the film *Speed*: if the water level drops below the tin, there is a chance the tin will explode, painting you and your kitchen in boiling caramel, except Keanu probably won't be there to save you). Remove from the heat and leave the tin to cool in the water for 1 hour. Remove the tin from the water and set aside to cool overnight.

2. Combine the lime zest and chilli flakes in a small bowl.

3. Melt the butter in a small saucepan then add the Cointreau and brown sugar. Cook over medium heat for 3–4 minutes until the sugar is dissolved and the sauce has thickened.

4. Heat a griddle pan over high heat until smoking.

5. Brush the pineapple slices with the Cointreau glaze and carefully place in the pan. Cook over high heat for 2–3 minutes until char lines appear then flip the pineapple over. Brush with more glaze and cook for a further 2–3 minutes. The pineapple should be soft and caramelised.

6. Place the slices of brioche in a dry frying pan over medium heat and gently toast on both sides.

7. Spread a very thick layer of dulce de leche on the brioche and top with a pineapple ring. Sprinkle over a little lime zest and chilli and garnish with coconut flakes.

If you have never made your own dulce de leche, we really encourage you to try it. It's ridiculously easy and you're left with the most beautiful creamy caramel that, quite frankly, is impossible to resist. After writing this recipe I was caught several times red-handed eating it straight from the tin. It will not last long!

08

BASICS

Every sandwich needs a little something extra, so here we have lovingly compiled our favourite fillings that add crunch, cream, texture and bite.

We have recently developed a possibly unhealthy love affair with pickles. Not only are they good for you, they pair brilliantly with with so many ingredients, it would have been remiss of us not to give them their own special place. Quick to make and long-lasting, they won't stay in the fridge for long.

The guac', slaw and sauces are staples in our house and should definitely not be limited to the sandwiches in this book. We picked up the guac' recipe in Mexico, so it is truly authentic (and the best you will taste). The coleslaw recipe is Lucy's Mum's, so no contest.

ALL THE PICKLES IN THE WORLD...

Pickles! Crunchy, sweet, tangy, sharp, addictive, you can do so much more with a pickle than just put it in a sandwich! (Now, now, let's keep it clean.) The below recipes will make more than you will need for two sandwiches, but they keep well in the fridge and can be used to accompany any number of dishes. Get your pickle on!

DILL PICKLES

MAKES 500 G (1 LB 2 OZ)

8 (about 500 g/1 lb 2 oz) baby cucumbers (qukes), trimmed

1 teaspoon whole black peppercorns

2 garlic cloves, peeled and thinly sliced

3–4 dill fronds

250 ml (8½ fl oz/1 cup) white vinegar

55 g (2 oz/¼ cup) sugar

3 tablespoons sea salt flakes

1. Wash the cucumbers well and pat dry with paper towel. Pack them into a large sterilised glass jar along with the peppercorns, garlic and dill.

2. Place the vinegar, sugar, salt and 250 ml (8½ fl oz/1 cup) water in a saucepan and bring to the boil. Leave to boil for 2–3 minutes, stirring until the sugar dissolves, then remove from the heat and pour into the jar, covering the cucumbers completely.

3. Seal the jar and set aside to cool to room temperature, then transfer to the fridge.

4. The pickles can be eaten after 2–3 days, and will keep for up to 2 weeks in the fridge.

PICKLED BEETROOT

MAKES 500 G (1 LB 2 OZ)

1 medium-sized beetroot

125 ml (4 fl oz/½ cup) white vinegar

2 tablespoons sugar

½ teaspoon salt

4 whole black peppercorns

4 coriander seeds

pinch of yellow mustard seeds

1 bay leaf

1. Bring a small saucepan of water to the boil and add the beetroot. Simmer for 30 minutes or until just tender. Drain and set aside to cool.

2. Meanwhile, combine the remaining ingredients and 2 tablespoons water in a small saucepan and bring to the boil. Simmer for a few minutes, stirring occasionally, until the sugar dissolves.

3. Peel the beetroot (wear kitchen gloves if you don't want pink digits) and cut into thin slices. Transfer to a sterilised glass jar and pour the hot pickling liquid over the top. Pop the lid on and set aside in the fridge for at least 3 hours, but preferably overnight.

4. The beetroot will keep for up to 2 weeks in the fridge.

PICKLED TURNIPS

MAKES 450 G (1 LB)

1–2 slices beetroot

450 g (1 lb) turnip, sliced into batons, about 1 cm (½ in) thick

1 bay leaf

150 ml (5 fl oz) white vinegar

1 tablespoon salt

½ teaspoon sugar

1. Place the beetroot in a large sterilised glass jar, and add the turnip, gently pushing down so they are tightly packed. Add the bay leaf.

2. Combine the remaining ingredients and 300 ml (10 fl oz) water in a small saucepan and bring to the boil. Simmer for a few minutes, stirring occasionally, until the sugar dissolves.

3. Pour enough hot pickling liquid over the turnips to completely cover them. Pop the lid on and leave to cool to room temperature before transferring to the fridge.

4. The pickled turnips will take 1 week to reach maximum flavour and will keep for up to 4 weeks in the fridge.

PICKLED RED ONION

MAKES 300 G (10½ OZ)

115 g (4 oz/½ cup) caster (superfine) sugar

125 ml (4 fl oz/½ cup) white vinegar

½ teaspoon salt

1 large red onion, thinly sliced

1. Combine the sugar, vinegar, salt and 170 ml (5½ fl oz/⅔ cup) water in a small saucepan and bring to the boil. Simmer for a few minutes, stirring occasionally, until the sugar dissolves.

2. Place the onion in a sterilised glass jar and pour the hot pickling liquid over the top. Seal the jar and set aside in the fridge for at least 3 hours or preferably overnight.

3. The pickled onion will keep for up to 1 week in the fridge.

PICKLED DAIKON & CARROT

MAKES 200 G (7 OZ)

115 g (4 oz/½ cup) caster (superfine) sugar

125 ml (4 fl oz/½ cup) rice wine vinegar or white vinegar

½ teaspoon salt

100 g (3½ oz) daikon, sliced into batons

100 g (3½ oz) carrot, sliced into batons

1. Combine the sugar, vinegar, salt and 170 ml (5½ fl oz/⅔ cup) water in a small saucepan and bring to the boil. Simmer for a few minutes, stirring occasionally, until the sugar dissolves.

2. Place the daikon and carrot into a large sterilised glass jar and pour the hot pickling liquid over the top. Seal the jar and set aside in the fridge for at least 3 hours or preferably overnight.

3. The pickles will keep for up to 2 weeks in the fridge.

No cookbook would be complete without a few extra bits and bobs at the end, which not only feature in this book but are also the perfect accompaniments to pretty much anything.

AND FINALLY...

GUACAMOLE

SERVES 2

¼ white onion, finely chopped

1 avocado

juice of 1 lime

small handful coriander (cilantro), finely chopped

½ teaspoon salt

1. Soak the white onion in a small bowl of cold water for 10 minutes to remove the harshness of the flavour. Drain.

2. Smash the avocado with the back of a fork in a small bowl. Add the onion along with the remaining ingredients and a little black pepper. Mix well until completely combined.

3. Preferably serve immediately. Although the guac' will discolour fairly quickly, we find you can just about get away with keeping it for 24 hours in the fridge before you're left with a '70s hue.

COLESLAW

SERVES 4

1 carrot, grated

¼ white or red cabbage or a mixture of both, shredded

2 spring onions (scallions), thinly sliced

2 tablespoons whole egg mayonnaise

squeeze of lemon juice

1. Combine the carrot, cabbage, spring onion and mayonnaise in a small bowl. Season with salt and pepper and add lemon juice to taste.

2. Coleslaw is best eaten on the day it is made, but it will keep in an airtight container in the fridge for up to 48 hours. Just remember to give everything a good stir as the dressing tends to pool and loiter at the bottom.

TAHINI SAUCE

MAKES 150 ML (5 FL OZ)

65 g (2¼ oz/¼ cup) tahini

juice of 1 lemon

1 garlic clove, finely chopped

1. Combine all of the ingredients in a small jar along with a large pinch of salt and 90 ml (3 fl oz) water. Put the lid on and shake well. You may have to encourage the tahini to loosen with a spoon – the end consistency should be of very runny yoghurt.

2. Tahini sauce will keep for 3–4 days in the fridge.

BARBECUE SAUCE

MAKES 300 G (10½ OZ)

115 g (4 oz/½ cup) dark brown sugar

375 ml (12½ fl oz/1½ cups) apple cider vinegar

120 g (4½ oz) tomato ketchup

2 tablespoons smoked paprika

1 teaspoon chilli flakes

3 tablespoons Worcestershire sauce

1. Combine all of the ingredients in a small saucepan and bring to the boil. Reduce the heat to low and cook for about 30 minutes, until thick and glossy. Season with salt and pepper to taste.

2. Barbecue sauce will keep in an airtight container in the fridge for up to 1 week.

INDEX

Published in 2017 by Smith Street Books
Melbourne | Australia
smithstreetbooks.com

ISBN: 978 1 92541 828 6

CIP data is available from the National Library of Australia.

Publisher: Paul McNally
Senior editor: Lucy Heaver, Tusk studio
Cover designers: Murray Batten, Sarah K James and Lucy Heaver
Designer: Murray Batten
Photographer: Chris Middleton
Stylist: Vicki Valsamis
Home economist: Jemima Good

Printed & bound in China by C&C Offset Printing Co., Ltd.

Book 23
10 9 8 7 6 5 4 3 2 1